WORLD

Meet the World 2023

English through Newspapers

Edited with Notes

by

Yasuhiko Wakaari

写真提供

AP/アフロ

読売新聞社

高砂電気工業株式会社

音声ファイルのダウンロード／ストリーミング

CD マーク表示がある箇所は、音声を弊社 HP より無料でダウンロード／ストリーミングすることができます。下記 URL の書籍詳細ページに音声ダウンロードアイコンがございますのでそちらから自習用音声としてご活用ください。

http://seibido.co.jp/ad669

Meet the World 2023
English through Newspapers

はしがき

● はじめに

　この教科書を手にしたみなさんの中には、「テレビやインターネット、スマホがあるこの時代になぜわざわざ新聞を読まなくてはいけないの？」と疑問に思う人がいるかもしれません。確かにテレビは新聞と比べて娯楽性や臨場感に優れていますし、インターネットには膨大な情報量とこれまでのメディアにはなかった「双方向性」があります。また携帯電話やスマートフォンの普及によって、世間の注目を集める試合や選挙の結果はほぼリアルタイムで、しかも検索しなくても分かるようになりました。

　では新聞はもう必要ないのでしょうか。いいえ、決してそんなことはありません。情報技術が発達した現在だからこそ、実は新聞が必要なのではないでしょうか。

　みなさんがすでに普段の生活で体験しているように、現代社会にはさまざまな情報があふれています。例えばインターネットの検索エンジンに「英字新聞」と入力すると281万件が、「新聞」に至っては8億800万件がヒットします。

　このように情報が氾濫している状況では、情報の取捨選択を行い、選択した情報に基づいて行動することが必要になります。では情報の取捨選択で一番大切なことは何でしょうか。

　これについてはさまざまな意見があるかもしれませんが、情報で最も重要なのはその「信頼性」だと思います。いくら早く手に入れることができても、信頼性に欠ける情報であればそれを基に行動するのは危険と言えます。福島第一原発の事故や新型コロナウイルスの感染拡大、ワクチンの接種が始まった時期に流れたさまざまな情報はそのことを私たちに教えてくれたのではないでしょうか。

　新聞は、現在の多様化したメディアの中で、最も信頼性が高いことが各種調査で明らかになっています。他のメディアに比べ記録性に優れていることがその証拠と言えるでしょう。新聞を読み、信頼性の高い情報を基に行動する習慣を身に付けることは、みなさんがこれから自分の将来を選択する上で極めて重要になります。

本書の目的と特徴

　本書は「英語はある程度読めるけれど英字新聞はほとんど読んだことがない」という方を対象とした教材です。本書の目的は3つあります。一つは英字新聞に慣れ親しんでもらうこと、もう一つは英字新聞を読むためのノウハウを身に付けてもらうこと、そして最後にみなさんの身のまわりで起こっているさまざまな出来事に興味を持ってもらうことです。それぞれの目的に関して本書で工夫した点をいくつか紹介します。

● ① 英字新聞に慣れ親しんでもらうこと

　みなさんは英語の文章を訳したときに「なんとか日本語にできたけど内容はほとんど分からなかった」という経験をしたことはないでしょうか。これにはいくつかの理由がありますが、「文

章の背景状況が分からない」ことが大きな要因として考えられます。

　本書では、Before reading において記事と関連する情報を提示したり、記事を理解する上で重要な語句を確認するタスクを設けています。これらのタスクを行うことで、「内容に関する背景知識があれば、英文記事の内容理解はそれほど難しくない」ことが実感できるでしょう。また収録した記事は、語数を基本にしつつ、トピックや場面のわかりやすさにも配慮して配列しています。本書での学習を通じて、最初は「長い」と感じていた記事にもいつの間にか抵抗なく取り組めるでしょう。

• ② 英字新聞を読むためのノウハウを身につけてもらうこと

　英字新聞の理解には、内容に関する背景知識の理解に加え、記事の形式、つまり新聞英語の構成や特徴の理解も重要です。

　本書ではみなさんにこのようなノウハウを身につけてもらうために、新聞英語の特徴を要点ごとにコラムにまとめ、本書の Unit 1 ～ 10 で紹介しています。またコラムの内容理解を助けるためのタスクを設け、記事を読みながら形式について少しずつ理解できるよう配慮しました。さらに巻頭の iii ～ v では新聞英語の特徴をまとめて掲載しています。

• ③ 現在の社会で起こっている様々な出来事に興味を持ってもらうこと

　本書では、現在の社会で起こっているさまざまな出来事に目を向けることができるよう、*The Japan News* 紙等から日本で起きた出来事と海外発の記事をバランスよく収録しています。またこの種の教材としては多めの 20 の記事を収録しました。特にオンラインでの体験や人工知能の活用など、みなさんの現在や今後の生活に関わる話題を多く取り上げています。

　もし本書の中にみなさんの興味を引く記事を見つけたら、ぜひ関連する情報を調べてみてください。記事に関する知識が深まると同時に、もっと多くのことを知りたいと思うようになるでしょう。そういう興味・関心を持つことがみなさんの将来の進路を決める意外なきっかけになるかもしれません。

• おわりに

　本書の作成にあたっては多くの方のご協力をいただきました。秋田大学の学生のみなさんには有益なアドバイスを、また成美堂の中澤ひろ子氏をはじめとするスタッフの方々にも大変お世話になりました。この場をお借りして厚くお礼申し上げます。

編著者記す

新聞英語の特徴

• いろいろな読み方に対応した記事の構成

　本や雑誌に比べ、新聞はいろいろな読み方をされます。時間をかけて全ての記事を熟読することもあれば、特定の記事だけを読んだり、記事の最初の部分にさっと目を通すだけのこともあります。新聞記事は最初の部分しか読まなくても要点が把握できるよう、Headline（見出し）、Lead（前文）、Body（本文）の3つで構成されています。

• **Headline** の特徴① スペースの効率的利用

　広告のコピーライティングと同様、新聞記事の Headline は、「短く、鋭く、気の利いた」（Short, Sharp, Snappy）表現で読者の目を引くように、また限られたスペースでもメッセージを効率的に伝えられるようにさまざまな工夫をしています。例えば、①冠詞、②特別動詞（BE, HAVE）、③接続詞（and, that）、④文の終わりのピリオド、といったメッセージの意味内容に大きく関わらない語や記号は基本的に省略されます。また、⑤略語、⑥縮約語、⑦つづりの短い語、のような省スペースの表現が多用されます。

• **Headline** の特徴② 時制の変化

　Headline では is, were といった BE 動詞や has, had のような HAVE 動詞が省略されるなど、通常の英語とは異なった時制表現が用いられます。具体的には、①「現在完了」の表現と「過去形」は「現在形」に、②「受身」の表現は「過去分詞」だけに、③「BE 動詞 + 現在分詞 (-ing)」（進行中、または現在から見て実現の可能性が極めて高いことを示す表現）は「現在分詞 (-ing)」だけに、④「BE 動詞 +going to+ 動詞の原形」（現時点で可能性が高いことを示す表現）は「to+動詞の原形」だけになります。

通常の英語では	新聞英語では
過去形	現在形
[HAVE] + 過去分詞	
[BE] + 過去分詞	過去分詞
[HAVE] been + 過去分詞	
[BE] + 現在分詞	現在分詞
[BE] + going to + 動詞の原形	to +動詞の原形

• Headline の特徴③ 句読点の使用

　すでに述べたように、Headline では and, that といった接続詞が省略され、代わりにコンマ (,) が使われます。またコロン (:) やセミコロン (;) にも接続詞や一部の前置詞の代わりをする働きがあります。コロンは誰かの発言や補足説明、セミコロンは前半部分と後半部分が何らかのつながりを持っていることを示します。具体的には、前半の内容について後半でその理由を挙げて説明したり、前半と後半の内容が対照的であることなどを意味します。

• Headline の特徴④ 略語、縮約語の使用

　すでに述べたように、Headline では IMF, NATO, IOC, WHO のような略語や、Dept., S'pore といった縮約語が多用されます。縮約語は Dept. や ad. のように語の最後にピリオド (.) がついたり、S'pore や int'l のようにアポストロフィ (') がつくことが多く、読み手はそれらの記号によって縮約語であると知ることができます。しかし記事によっては dept や intl のように、そのような記号さえも省略されることがあります。

• Headline の特徴⑤ つづりの短い語の使用

　同じような意味を表わす語が 2 つ以上ある場合、Headline ではつづりの短い方を用います。例えば「援助する」の意味を表わす語には aid や assist、「問題」には issue や problem などの語がありますが、新聞英語では特別な事情がない限り短い方の aid や issue が使用されます。

• Headline の特徴⑥ 簡潔な表現の問題点

　すでに述べたように、Headline ではメッセージの意味内容と大きく関連しない機能語（例：特別動詞や接続詞）を省略したり、省スペースの表現（例：縮約語やつづりの短い語）を多用するなど、メッセージを効率的に示す工夫をしています。他方で、機能語の省略や省スペース表現の多用はいろいろな解釈を可能にするという問題を伴います。例えば新聞英語の現在形は過去形と現在完了の両方の解釈ができます。また Rep. という縮約語は Republican（[米国の]共和党員）にも Representative（[米国の] 下院議員）にも解釈できます。こういった場合の判断には Headline 全体またはその先の Lead や Body まで読むことが重要です。

• Lead の特徴

　記事全文のうち最初の部分を Lead（前文）と言います。Lead は記事の書き出しであると同時に記事全文の要約でもあります。Lead には「5W1H」、つまり Who, What, When, Where, Why, How（誰が、何を、いつ、どこで、なぜ、どのように）に関する情報が簡潔に含まれていて、この部分を読むだけで記事の要旨が理解できます。Lead は読み手、特に記事に最後まで目を通す時間のない人にとって大切な役割を担っています。

• Body の特徴

　記事全文のうち Lead を除く部分を Body（本文）と言います。Body は通常複数の段落から構成され、Headline や Lead で示された要点を詳しく説明する役割を担っています。Body の段落は情報の核心部分（＝重要度が高い部分）から順に配列され、段落が下がるに従って補足的、周辺的（＝重要度が低い）になっていきます。このような段落構成を「逆三角形型」または「逆ピラミッド型」（inverted pyramid style）と呼びますが、この構成は読み手にとって情報を効率的に把握できるメリットが、書き手にとっては記事の分量を調整する際に書き直す手間が省けるメリットがあります。

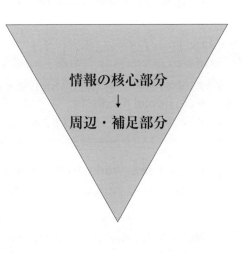

• その他の新聞英語の特徴

　新聞英語に見られるその他の特徴として、次の 2 つを挙げることができます。

① 発言者・報告者の名前は発言や報告内容の後に置かれることが多い。

　　　例 1：South Africa's legal lion breeding..., <u>an animal welfare group warned</u>....

　　　例 2：Tigers are not native to South Africa and..., <u>the organization said</u>.

② 補足説明の挿入が多い。

　　　例 1：the renowned Egyptologist Zahi Hawass, <u>a former anitiquities minister</u>, the....

　　　例 2：The mummy discovered in Luxor, <u>Southern Egypt</u>, is the only one not....

これらの特徴は、限られたスペースの中で読み手が効率的に要点を把握できるよう配慮した結果生まれたと考えられます。

■ CONTENTS

Unit の構成

　本書は、リーディングを中心に、リスニングやスピーキング、ライティングなどの技能を総合的に育成することをねらいとしており、各 Unit は Before reading 1 及び 2, While reading 1 〜 5, After reading 1 〜 3 の 10 のタスクで構成されています。それぞれのタスクのねらいは以下の通りです。

・Before reading 1： 背景知識を与えることでトピックに対する興味や理解を促したり、トピックと関連する語句を確認するタスク。
・Before reading 2： 専門用語のように、文脈からの推測も難しい語句などの意味を確認するタスク。

・While reading 1： 情報を整理するノート・テイキングのタスク。
・While reading 2： 文章から特定の情報を探し出す、スキャニングのタスク。
・While reading 3： 文章の要点をすくい取って全体の大意を理解する、スキミングを意識した要約完成のタスク。
・While reading 4： CD を聞き、完成した要約や全体の大意を確認するリスニングのタスク。
・While reading 5： 行間を読み取らせる推論発問により読解力を高めるタスク。

・After reading 1： 語句を並べ替える英作文により文法力を鍛えるタスク。
・After reading 2： 定義をヒントに文中から単語を抜き出すことで語の意味を確認するタスク。
・After reading 3： 記事のトピックに関する考えを深めると同時に、自分の意見やアイデアをメモにまとめることでライティングの力を養うタスク。メモを参考に口頭で発表することでスピーキングの力を高めることにもつながります。

コラム

UNIT 1

75% of 3rd-year junior high school students get news from social media

中3の75%、SNSからニュースを入手

 みなさんはどんなメディアからニュースを得ていますか？ メディアの多様化によって、新聞やテレビからではなく、SNSからニュースを入手する人が増えています。このUnitでは、中学生の多くがSNSからニュースを得ていることを報じた記事を取り上げます。

🔲 Before reading 1

説明を読み、内容に関する理解を深めましょう。
また図からどんなことが言えるか考えましょう。

- 記事の調査は読売新聞社と電通総研（Dentsu Institute）によって実施され（conducted）ました。

- この調査によると、情報源（source of news）を信頼に値する（trustworthy）と答えた小学生（elementary school students）と中学生の割合は半数近くに上っています。

- 株式会社ICT総研がまとめた「2021年モバイルニュースアプリ市場動向調査」によると、

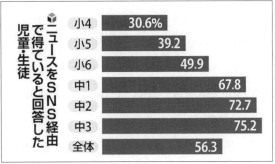

ニュースをSNS経由で得ていると回答した児童・生徒

小4	30.6%
小5	39.2
小6	49.9
中1	67.8
中2	72.7
中3	75.2
全体	56.3

出典：読売新聞社　2022年1月27日

ニュースを入手する媒体は、新聞・雑誌などの紙媒体から、パソコン上のニュースサイトを経て、現在はモバイルニュースアプリが主流になっており、日本国内におけるこのアプリの利用者数は5,671万人と増加が続いています。

🔲 Before reading 2

日本語に対応する英語表現を選択肢から選び、○で囲みましょう。

1. 調査　　　　　　　survey / surveil

2. 態度　　　　　　　altitude / attitude

3. 回答者　　　　　　respondant / respondent

4. 多様化　　　　　　devitalization / diversification

5. 充満して、多い　　rife / rive

75% of 3rd-year junior high school students get news from social media

① Three in four students in the third year of junior high school get news from social media, according to a survey by The Yomiuri Shimbun and Dentsu Institute.

② The survey was conducted from September to October on about 6,300 students in the fourth year of elementary school to the third year of junior high school at 42 schools cooperating with the Yomiuri Education Network.

③ According to the survey, 56.3% of all respondents get their news via smartphones or other devices, and 47% do not check the source of news.

④ The survey was conducted to find out how the diversification of media has changed children's attitudes toward news.

⑤ By school year, the percentage of respondents who said they get their news from social media was highest among third-year junior high school students, at 75.2%, and lowest among fourth-year elementary school students, at 30.6%.

⑥ The higher the school year, the higher the percentage.

⑦ Asked whether they check the source of online news stories, 43.1% of fourth-year elementary school students and 47.7% of third-year junior high school students said they did not.

⑧ More junior high school students than elementary school students said they did check the source. Among third-year junior high schoolers, 49.0% checked the source, the highest percentage over all year groups.

写真：ペイレスイメージズ / アフロ

Yomiuri Education Network 読売新聞教育ネットワーク

⑨ Almost half of the students said news from social media is "trustworthy" or "more or less trustworthy," averaging 48.9% among all respondents.

35 ⑩ "Children don't really feel that they can be deceived by information on the internet," said a professor of Tokyo Woman's Christian University, who is knowledgeable about problems regarding smartphone use by children. "It is important to teach elementary and junior high school students that the internet is rife with fake news and

40 inaccurate information."

Tokyo Woman's Christian University 東京女子大学

⊛ *While reading* ❶ 次に関して、記事を読んで分かったことをメモしてみましょう。

1. 調査の目的、実施時期及び回答者について

....

....

2. SNS でニュースを入手すると回答した児童・生徒の割合

....

....

3. ネット情報の発信源を確認すると回答した児童・生徒の割合

....

....

4. 東京女子大学の教授の発言

....

....

📃 column　｜いろいろな読み方に対応した記事の構成

本や雑誌に比べ、新聞はいろいろな読み方をされます。時間をかけて全ての記事を熟読することもあれば、特定の記事だけを読んだり、記事の最初の部分にさっと目を通すだけのこともあります。新聞記事は最初の部分しか読まなくても要点が把握できるよう、Headline（見出し）、Lead（前文）、Body（本文）の3つで構成されています。

Task この Unit の記事の Headline、Lead、Body をそれぞれ○で囲みましょう。

While reading 2　記事の中で次の情報が述べられている段落の番号を書きましょう。

1. 調査対象となった学校の数：[　　　]

2. SNSからニュースを入手すると回答した小学4年生の割合：[　　　]

3. ネットニュースの情報源を確認していないと回答した小学4年生の割合：[　　　]

4. SNSのニュースを「信じられる」「だいたい信じられる」と回答した人の割合：[　　　]

While reading 3　空欄に適切な単語または数字を入れ、記事の要約を完成させましょう。答えが単語の場合、最初の文字がヒントとして示してあります。

In order to find out how the diversification of media has changed children's
1)a_____ toward news, a survey was conducted from September to
October on about 2)_____ students in the fourth year of elementary school
to the third year of junior high school. According to the survey, 56.3% of all
respondents get their news via smartphones or other 3)d_____, and 47% do
not check the news source. In addition, 48.9% of the students said news from
4)s_____ media is "trustworthy" or "more or less trustworthy," which shows
that children don't really feel that they can be deceived by information on the
5)i_____.

While reading 4　3で空欄に入れた単語または数字が正しいか、音声で確認しましょう。

🔊 1-07

While reading 5　記事が示唆する内容と合致すればT、しなければFを記入しましょう。

1. The percentage of the third-year junior high schoolers who get news from
   social media was more than double that of the fourth-year elementary
   schoolers.　[　　　]

2. The percentage of fifth-year elementary schoolers who get news from social
   media was higher than that of sixth-year elementary schoolers.　[　　　]

3. The percentage of fourth-year elementary schoolers who do not check the
   news source was higher than the average of all respondents.　[　　　]

4. The percentage of third-year junior high schoolers who checked the news
   source was higher than that of second-year junior high schoolers.　[　　　]

 **After reading 1** 　語句を並べ替えて英文を完成させましょう。間違った場合、解答欄に正しい答えを書くこと。なお文頭に来る語句も小文字にしてあります。

1. その調査は 42 の学校で学ぶ約 6,300 人の児童・生徒に対して実施された。

(at / on / was / conducted / the survey / about 6,300 students) 42 schools.

予 想 : ....

....

解 答 : ....

　　　　　　　　　42 schools.

2. 回答者たちは彼らが情報源を確認するかどうかを尋ねられた。

The respondents (they / were / asked / check / whether / the source) of news.

予 想 : ....

....

解 答 : *The respondents* ....

　　　　　　　　of news.

3. 子どもは自分たちがネット情報にだまされる可能性があることを学ぶべきだ。

Children should learn that they (be / by / on / can / deceived / information) the internet.

予 想 : ....

....

解 答 : *Children should learn that they* ....

　　　　　　　　the internet.

4. ネットがフェイクニュースで溢れていることを中学生に教えるのは重要だ。

It is (to / that / teach / important / the internet / junior high school students) is rife with fake news.

予 想 : ....

....

解 答 : *It is* ....

　　　　　　　　is rife with fake news.

5

次の説明はどの語についてのものか、文中から抜き出して必要に応じ正しい形に直しましょう。最初の文字がヒントとして示してあります。

1. a set of questions that you ask a large number of people in order to find out about their opinions or behavior

2. an organization that has a particular purpose such as scientific or educational work, or the building where this organization is based

3. to do something in order to find out whether something really is correct, true, or in good condition

4. the opinions and feelings that you usually have about something, especially when this is shown in your behavior

5. to give someone a wrong belief or opinion about something

6. made to look like something else

1. s _____	2. i _____	3. c _____
4. a _____	5. d _____	6. f _____

次の課題について、自分の考えを述べましょう。

ネット情報の信頼性に関する問題を小学生に知ってもらうために、あなたはどのような伝え方をしますか。またその伝え方を選んだ理由は何ですか。あなたの考えを書いてみましょう。

日本語でのメモ

英語での作文

UNIT 2

Nagoya firm works to brew beer that's out of this world

名古屋の会社、この世にないビールの醸造に取り組む

もし将来宇宙旅行が身近になったとしたら、みなさんは宇宙でビールを飲んでみたいと思いますか？ この Unit では、ビール生産の実績がない状況で宇宙でのビール醸造に挑戦する名古屋の会社の取り組みを報じた記事を取り上げます。

🔲 Before reading 1

説明を読み、内容に関する理解を深めましょう。
また図からどんなことが言えるか考えましょう。

- ビールは、麦芽（malt）から作った麦汁（wort）を酵母（yeast）を使って発酵させる（ferment）ことで醸造され（brewed）ます。
- 無重力環境での発酵には、液体内で人工的に（artificially）対流（convective flow）を発生させる必要があります。

各国ロケット打上げベンチマーク (2019 年 12 月末現在)

各国ロケット	打上げ成功率	オンタイム率
H-IIA/B (日)	98.0% (48/49)	83.3%
デルタ4 (米)	97.5% (39/40)	43.8%
アトラス5 (米)	98.8% (82/83)	65.8%
ファルコン9 (米)	97.6% (80/82)	48.8%
アリアン5 (欧)	96.3% (104/108)	71.6%
プロトンM (露)	89.8% (97/108)	
ゼニット3 (露)	91.3% (42/46)	
長征3 (中)	95.1% (117/123)	

(c) 宇宙航空研究開発機構 (JAXA)

🔲 Before reading 2

日本語に対応する英語表現を選択肢から選び、○で囲みましょう。

1. 宇宙飛行士　　　　　　astronaut / astrologist

2. 無重力　　　　　　　　zero glavity / zero gravity

3. 精密機器　　　　　　　precisian machinery / precision machinery

4. 実証実験　　　　　　　demolition experiment / demonstration experiment

5. 宇宙航空研究開発機構　Japan Aerospace Xenophilia Agency /

　　　　　　　　　　　　Japan Aerospace Exploration Agency

Nagoya firm works to brew beer that's out of this world

① A Nagoya-based precision machinery maker is working on technology for brewing out-of-this-world beer.

② Eyeing a future when people will stay in outer space for longer periods than now, the company said it aims to make it possible to produce fermented foods on the International Space Station or in other off-planet environments.

③ Takasago Electric Inc. was in charge of developing devices related to a cell-cultivation experiment that an astronaut carried out while aboard the ISS as part of a Japan Aerospace Exploration Agency project.

④ Although the company has never produced beer, it has taken on the space-related challenge.

⑤ Beer is brewed by fermenting sweet wort made from malt using yeast. If the fermentation takes place in almost zero gravity, such as inside the ISS, it is necessary to artificially create convective flows in the liquid to be successful.

⑥ Late last year, the company test-produced a palm-size automatic beer brewing machine that can control the amount of gases discharged during the fermenting process.

⑦ Takasago Electric plans to confirm the technological capability of the machine by carrying out a demonstration experiment around spring.

⑧ The company aims to further downsize its machine and put one on a rocket to be launched in 2024 to conduct experimental brewing.

写真提供：高砂電気工業株式会社

out-of-this-world
奇想天外の、現世離れした

International Space Station　国際宇宙ステーション

Takasago Electric Inc.
高砂電気工業

ISS International Space Station の略称

8

⑨ Also, the company plans to bring back yeast grown in space to Earth and then produce a space-branded beer.

⑩ If space travel and stays in space increase, technologies to improve the quality of clothing, food and quarters will be necessary.

quarters 住居

⑪ Expecting the demand for alcoholic beverages and fermented foods in space to increase, the company aims to develop technologies for mass-producing such products.

alcoholic beverage
アルコール飲料

⑫ The managing director of the company said, "We aim to make it possible in 2030 for people in space to drink beer brewed in space."

While reading 1 次に関して、記事を読んで分かったことをメモしてみましょう。

1. 高砂電気工業について

....

....

2. 宇宙旅行や宇宙での滞在期間の増加に伴って想定される需要

....

....

3. 高砂電気工業が今後予定している取り組み

....

....

≣ column **Headline の特徴①スペースの効率的利用**

広告のコピーライティングと同様、新聞記事の Headline は「短く、鋭く、気の利いた」(Short, Sharp, Snappy) 表現で読者の目を引くように、また限られたスペースでメッセージを最も効率的に伝えられるようにさまざまな工夫をしています。例えば、①冠詞、②特別動詞 (BE, HAVE)、③接続詞 (and, that)、④文の終わりのピリオド、といったメッセージの意味・内容に大きく関わらない語や記号は基本的に省略されます。また、⑤略語、⑥縮約語、⑦つづりの短い語、のような省スペースの表現が多用されます。

Task 次の3つの Headline を分析し、基になる英文を作ってみましょう。

(1) 7 Earth-size planets found
(2) Lack of oxygen hurting corals in world's oceans
(3) DiCaprio, pope discuss environment

⊘ While reading 2

記事の中で次の情報が述べられている段落の番号を書きましょう。

1. 高砂電気工業の本社がある場所：[　　　　]

2. 手のひらサイズのビール自動醸造機が試作された時期：[　　　　]

3. さらに小型化した自動醸造機が搭載されるロケットの打ち上げ予定時期：[　　　　]

4. 高砂電気工業の会長のコメント：[　　　　]

⊘ While reading 3

空欄に適切な単語または数字を入れ、記事の要約を完成させましょう。
答えが単語の場合、最初の文字がヒントとして示してあります。

Takasago Electric Inc., a Nagoya-based ¹⁾p_____ machinery maker, is working on technology for brewing out-of-this-world beer. Late in 2021, the company test-produced a palm-size ²⁾a_____ beer brewing machine. It plans to confirm the technological capabilities of the machine by carrying out a ³⁾d_____ experiment around spring. The company also aims to further downsize its machine and put one on a rocket to be launched in ⁴⁾_____ to conduct experimental brewing. Furthermore, the company plans to bring back yeast grown in space to ⁵⁾E_____ and then produce a space-branded beer.

⊘ While reading 4

3 で空欄に入れた単語または数字が正しいか、音声で確認しましょう。

🔊 1-14

⊘ While reading 5

記事が示唆する内容と合致すれば T、しなければ F を記入しましょう。

1. Takasago Electric Inc. was involved in a Japan Aerospace Exploration Agency project.　[　　　　]

2. The ISS has a space with almost zero gravity inside.　[　　　　]

3. Takasago Electric Inc. test-produced a palm-size automatic beer brewing machine in the spring of 2021.　[　　　　]

4. Takasago Electric Inc. aims to make an automatic beer brewing machine smaller than our palm.　[　　　　]

 **After reading 1** 語句を並べ替えて英文を完成させましょう。間違った場合、解答欄に正しい答えを書くこと。

1. その会社は細胞培養実験の関連装置開発を担当した。

The company (in / of / was / charge / devices / developing) related to a cell-cultivation experiment.

予想： ....

解答： *The company*
related to a cell-cultivation experiment.

2. それは ISS での発酵食品生産を実現した。

It (it / to / made / produce / possible / fermented foods) on the ISS.

予想： ....

解答： *It*
on the ISS.

3. その会社は 2024 年に打ち上げ予定のロケットへの機械の搭載を目指している。

The company aims to (be / on / to / put / a rocket / the machine) launched in 2024.

予想： ....

解答： *The company aims to*
launched in 2024.

4. その会社は宇宙での発酵食品の需要増加を期待している。

The company (in / for / space / expects / the demand / fermented foods) to increase.

予想： ....

解答： *The company*
to increase.

1. the area beyond the Earth where the stars and planets are

2. to experience a chemical change because of the action of yeast or bacteria, often changing sugar to alcohol; to make something change in this way

3. grain, especially barley, that has been left in water for a period of time and then dried, used for making beer, whiskey, etc.

4. the force that causes something to fall to the ground or to be attracted to another planet

5. to send out gas, liquid, smoke, etc., or to allow it to escape

6. a vehicle used for travelling or carrying things into space, which is shaped like a big tube

1. s _____	2. f _____	3. m _____
4. g _____	5. d _____	6. r _____

After reading 3 次の課題について、自分の考えを述べましょう。

将来宇宙で長期間の滞在が可能になったら、そこでどんなものが必要になると思いますか。またそれが必要だと思う理由は何ですか。あなたの考えを書いてみましょう。

日本語でのメモ

英語での作文

UNIT 3

Not just for the elite— China's ex-athletes in school sport push

エリートのためだけでなく──中国の元選手、 学校スポーツの推進に関わる

もし学校の体育の授業でオリンピックのメダリストが指導してくれるとしたら、み なさんはどう思いますか。この Unit では、中国が学校でのスポーツ推進に取り組ん でいることを報じた記事を紹介します。この背景にはどんな状況があるのでしょう か。

⊞ Before reading 1

説明を読み、内容に関する理解を深めましょう。 また図からどんなことが言えるか考えましょう。

- 競争の激しい中国においては、スポーツはトッ プレベルの競技者（top-level competitor）のも ので、それ以外の人には時間の無駄（waste of time）と考えられていたようです。
- この Unit に登場する Sui さんは、国家スポーツ 育成機関（state sports machine）でエリート （elite）としての訓練を受けました。2011 年に世 界体操選手権種目別女子平均台を制して世界チャ ンピオン（world champion）となった他、ロン ドン五輪（London Olympics）では銀メダルも 獲得しています。

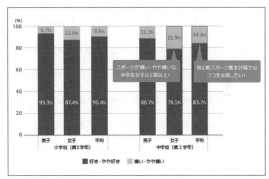

出典：スポーツ庁「平成 29 年度全国体力・運動能力、運動習 慣等調査」
(https://sports.go.jp/special/policy/new-curriculum-guideline.html)

⊞ Before reading 2

日本語に対応する英語表現を選択肢から選び、○で囲みましょう。

1. 体操選手　　　　　　gymel / gymnast

2. 元選手　　　　　　　ex-athlete / distinguished athlete

3. 胴　　　　　　　　　torso / torsade

4. 平均台　　　　　　　balance beam / balance stand

5. 奪い合い、混乱　　　scramble / scramjet

13

Not just for the elite—
China's ex-athletes in school sport push

①   Petite but commanding, China's former world champion gymnast Sui Lu stood among a sea of yoga mats doling out encouragement to her students as they bent their torsos towards their outstretched legs.

10   ② Sui was four years old when she was picked out by China's state sports machine and began training as an elite athlete. She became world champion on the balance beam in 2011 and won silver at the London Olympics the following year.

③ But the pupils taking instruction from her in the bright,

15   airy room in a Shanghai university harboured no such ambitions—Sui's class was on basic physical fitness.

④ Lessons taught by former top athletes are part of a recent government push to carve out more time for youth fitness in the world's most populous country, as it hopes to capitalise

20   on heightened enthusiasm for sport ahead of this month's Beijing Winter Olympics.

⑤ "People didn't like sports before. They were under pressure to study and didn't have time for exercise. But now everyone values sports," Sui told AFP, after running her students

25   through more stretches and balletic exercises.

⑥   The new state emphasis on exercise—schoolwork has been reduced, and targets such as a two-hour minimum of daily physical activity have been introduced—has forced a scramble to find qualified teachers.

30   ⑦ That has given Sui and other ex-athletes new career

写真：AFP/WAA

a sea of 〜
たくさんの〜
dole out 〜
〜を分け与える

harbo(u)r　心に抱く

Beijing Winter
Olympics　北京冬季五輪

options in a previously limited system.

⑧ "It's not like before when everyone thought professional athletes could only teach other professionals after retirement," Sui said.

35 ⑨ She sees her mission as not about creating elite—or even middling—athletes, but to break down Chinese perceptions that sport is only for top-level competitors and a waste of time for everyone else.

middling 並みの

🔗 While reading 1

次に関して、記事を読んで分かったことをメモしてみましょう。

1. Sui Lu さんについて

....

....

2. 人々がスポーツを好まなかった背景

....

....

3. 中国政府のスポーツに関する政策

....

....

📑 column   Headline の特徴② 時制の変化

Headline では is, were といった BE 動詞や has, had のような HAVE 動詞が省略されるなど、通常の英語とは異なった時制表現が用いられます。具体的には、①「現在完了」の表現と「過去形」は「現在形」に、②「受身」の表現は「過去分詞」だけに、③「BE 動詞＋現在分詞 (-ing)」（進行中、または現在から見て実現の可能性が極めて高いことを示す表現）は「現在分詞」に、④「BE 動詞＋going to＋動詞の原形」（現時点で可能性が高いことを示す表現）は「to＋動詞の原形」になります。

通常の英語では	新聞英語では
過去形	①
[HAVE] ＋ 過去分詞	
[BE] ＋ 過去分詞	②
[HAVE] been ＋ 過去分詞	
[BE] ＋ 現在分詞	③
[BE] ＋ going to ＋ 動詞の原形	④

Task　上の表の ①〜④に適切な表現を入れ、表を完成させましょう。

While reading 2 記事の中で次の情報が述べられている段落の番号を書きましょう。

1. スイさんが平均台で世界チャンピオンになった年： [　　　]

2. スイさんが体育の授業を担当している大学の名前： [　　　]

3. スイさんに取材を行った報道機関の名前： [　　　]

4. 中国政府が目標として定めた毎日の運動時間： [　　　]

While reading 3 空欄に適切な単語または数字を入れ、記事の要約を完成させましょう。
答えが単語の場合、最初の文字がヒントとして示してあります。

　　Sui Lu is a former world champion Chinese ¹⁾g_____. When she was four years old, she was picked out by China's state sports machine and began ²⁾t_____ as an elite athlete. She became world champion on the balance beam in ³⁾_____ and won silver at the London Olympics the following year. Now she teaches basic physical fitness in a Shanghai university. She sees her ⁴⁾m_____ as not about creating elite—or even middling—athletes, but to break down Chinese perceptions that sport is only for top-level ⁵⁾c_____ and a waste of time for everyone else.

While reading 4 3で空欄に入れた単語または数字が正しいか、音声で確認しましょう。

🔊 1-20

While reading 5 記事が示唆する内容と合致すれば T、しなければ F を記入しましょう。

1. The London Olympics was held in 2014.　[　　　]

2. Most of the students who Sui Lu teaches in a Shanghai university want to be elite athletes.　[　　　]

3. Students in China are encouraged to do physical activity for a total of more than 10 hours a week.　[　　　]

4. Before the state emphasis on exercise, it was unusual in China that ex-athletes taught non-athletes after retirement.　[　　　]

 **After reading 1** 　語句を並べ替えて英文を完成させましょう。間違った場合、解答欄に正しい答えを書くこと。

1. その学生たちには勉強の重圧があり、運動の時間がなかった。

The students were under pressure to study and (did / for / not / have / time / exercise).

予 想： ....

解 答： *The students were under pressure to study and* ....

....

2. 国家による運動の重視は資格のある教員を見つけるための混乱を生じさせた。

The state emphasis on exercise (to / has / find / forced / a scramble / qualified teachers).

予 想： ....

解 答： *The state emphasis on exercise* ....

....

3. スイさんは自身の使命について、エリート選手を作ることではないと考えている。

Sui (as / not / sees / about / creating / her mission) elite athletes.

予 想： ....
解 答： *Sui* .... *elite athletes.*

4. 彼女の使命は、スポーツは時間の無駄という中国人の見方を壊すことだ。

Her mission (is / to / down / that / break / Chinese perceptions) sport is a waste of time.

予 想： ....

....
解 答： *Her mission* ....

sport is a waste of time.

After reading 2　次の説明はどの語についてのものか、文中から抜き出して必要に応じ正しい形に直しましょう。最初の文字がヒントとして示してあります。

1. having the confidence to make people respect and obey you

2. a system of exercises that help you control your mind and body in order to relax

3. a situation in which people compete with and push each other in order to get what they want

4. the fact of stopping work because you have reached a particular age; the time when you do this

5. something that you feel you must do because it is your duty

6. a situation in which it is not worth spending time, money, etc., on something

1. c _____	2. y _____	3. s _____
4. r _____	5. m _____	6. w _____

After reading 3　次の課題について、自分の考えを述べましょう。

子どもの運動能力低下の問題を解決するために、どのような取り組みが必要だと思いますか。
またその取り組みが重要と思う理由は何ですか。あなたの考えを書いてみましょう。

日本語でのメモ

英語での作文

UNIT 4

Egypt 'digitally unwraps' mummy of famed pharaoh

エジプト、有名な王のミイラを「デジタル開封」

 みなさんはミイラの中身を見てみたいと思ったことはありますか？　このUnitでは、高度なX線技術やCTスキャンによって、直接触れることのない安全な方法でミイラのデジタル開封が行われたことを紹介した記事を取り上げます。

🔲 Before reading 1

説明を読み、内容に関する理解を深めましょう。
また図からどんなことが言えるか考えましょう。

- エジプト（Egypt）の観光・考古省（the tourism and antiquities ministry）によれば、今回のアメンホテプ1世（Amenhotep I）のミイラの「デジタル開封」を行ったのは放射線学（radiology）のサハル・サリーム教授（professor）と著名な（renowned）エジプト学者（Egyptologist）のザヒ・ハワス元観光・考古相の研究チームです。

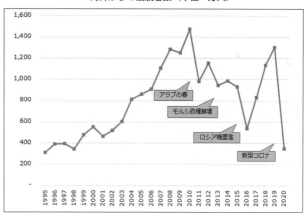

海外からの渡航者数（単位：万人）

出所：世界銀行、考古・観光省よりジェトロ作成
資料：ジェトロ「新型コロナ禍で観光業は（エジプト）（地域・分析レポート）」（2021年9月24日）

🔲 Before reading 2

日本語に対応する英語表現を選択肢から選び、○で囲みましょう。

1. 考古学者　　　　　archaeologist / anthropologist

2. 埋葬用マスク　　　funerary mask / funambulate mask

3. 再埋葬　　　　　　reberial / reburial

4. ミイラ化　　　　　mystification / mummification

5. 陰謀　　　　　　　conspiracy / inhabitation

Egypt 'digitally unwraps' mummy of famed pharaoh

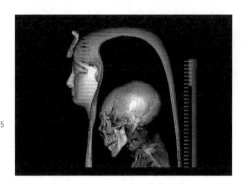

写真 : EGYPTIAN MINISTRY OF ANTIQUITIES / WAA

① Egypt has digitally unwrapped the mummy of famed Pharaoh Amenhotep I, revealing its secrets for the first time since it was discovered in 1881 without disturbing his funerary mask.

② Thanks to the advanced digital 3D imagery, researchers unearthed new mummification techniques used for the pharaoh whose rule dates back more than 1,500 BC.

thanks to 〜 〜のおかげで

③ The research was led by Sahar Saleem, a professor of radiology at Cairo University, and the renowned Egyptologist Zahi Hawass, a former antiquities minister, the tourism and antiquities ministry said in a statement Tuesday.

④ Saleem and Hawass used advanced X-ray technology, CT (computed tomography) scanning, as well as advanced computer software programs to digitally unwrap the mummy of Amenhotep I in a safe non-invasive method without the need to touch the mummy, it said.

X-ray　X線

⑤ The Egyptian study revealed for the first time the face of King Amenhotep I, his age, health condition, in addition to many secrets about the mummy's unique mummification and reburial.

⑥ Analysis showed Amenhotep I was the first pharaoh to be mummified with arms crossed and the last not to have had his brain removed from the skull.

⑦ The tomography scan revealed the pharaoh, who conducted several military campaigns during his 21-year rule, had died at the age of 35, apparently of injury or illness.

⑧ The mummy discovered in Luxor, southern Egypt, is the only one not to have had its tight bands unrolled by archaeologists, in order to preserve the mask and garlands of flowers that surround it like hair.

35　⑨ The same method of technical unwrapping, as described by Saleem, revealed in 2012 the harem conspiracy in which Ramses III had his throat slit, a conspiracy hatched by a wife seeking to have her son on the throne rather than the first-born of a rival.

 While reading 1　次に関して、記事を読んで分かったことをメモしてみましょう。

1.　アメンホテプ 1 世について

　...

　...

2.　ラムセス 3 世について

　...

　...

3.　分析で明らかになったこと

　...

　...

---

column　　**Headline の特徴③ 句読点の使用**

すでに述べたように、Headline では and, that といった接続詞が省略され、代わりにコンマ (,) が使われます。またコロン (:)、セミコロン (;) にも接続詞や一部の前置詞の代わりをする働きがあります。コロンは誰かの発言や補足説明、セミコロンは前半部分と後半部分が何らかのつながりを持っていることを示します。具体的には、前半の内容について後半でその理由を挙げて説明したり、前半と後半の内容が対照的であることなどを意味します。

Task　次の 3 つの記事の Headline にあるコロン (:) は何を表わしているか、考えてみましょう。

(1) Oxfam: 8 men as rich as half the world
(2) 'Vegetable steel' : Bamboo as ecologically-friendly building material
(3) U.K. court: Richard III to be buried in Leicester

While reading 2　記事の中で次の情報が述べられている段落の番号を書きましょう。

1. アメンホテプ１世のミイラが発見された年：[　　　]
2. サハル・サリーム教授が所属する大学の名前：[　　　]
3. アメンテホプ１世が亡くなった時の年齢：[　　　]
4. 2012年のデジタル開封の対象になったミイラ：[　　　]

While reading 3　空欄に適切な単語または数字を入れ、記事の要約を完成させましょう。答えが単語の場合、最初の文字がヒントとして示してあります。

Egypt has digitally unwrapped the mummy of famed Pharaoh Amenhotep I, revealing its secrets for the first time since it was discovered in **1)**_____ without disturbing his funerary mask. With the use of advanced X-ray technology, CT **2)**s_____, as well as advanced computer software programs, analysis showed Amenhotep I was the first pharaoh to be mummified with arms **3)**c_____ and the last not to have had his brain removed from the skull. The study also revealed the pharaoh, who conducted several **4)**m_____ campaigns during his 21-year rule, had died at the age of 35, apparently of injury or **5)**i_____ .

While reading 4　3で空欄に入れた単語または数字が正しいか、音声で確認しましょう。

🔊 1-26

While reading 5　記事が示唆する内容と合致すればT、しなければFを記入しましょう。

1. King Amenhotep I ruled Egypt more than 3,500 years ago.　[　　　]
2. Zahi Hawass is in charge of the tourism and antiquities ministry.　[　　　]
3. King Amenhotep I had ruled Egypt when he was 15 years old.　[　　　]
4. All the other mummies found in Luxor had their tight bands unrolled by archaeologists.　[　　　]

1. 新しいミイラ化の技術が、その治世が紀元前 1500 年より昔であった王に対して使われた。

New mummification techniques were used (for / back / rule / dates / whose / the pharaoh) more than 1,500 BC.

予想： ....

解答： *New mummification techniques were used*

more than 1,500 BC.

2. 彼は頭蓋骨から脳を取り出されなかった最後の王だった。

He was the last pharaoh not to (had / from / have / removed / his brain / the skull).

予想： ....

解答： *He was the last pharaoh not to*

3. 同じ方法はラムセス 3 世が喉を切られたハーレムでの陰謀を 2012 年に明らかにした。

The same method revealed in 2012 (in / had / which / his throat / Ramses III / the harem conspiracy) slit.

予想： ....

解答： *The same method revealed in 2012*

slit.

4. それは自分の息子を王座につけようと模索していた妻が企んだ。

It was (by / to / have / hatched / seeking / a wife) her son on the throne.

予想： ....

解答： *It was*

her son on the throne.

 **After reading 2**　次の説明はどの語についてのものか、文中から抜き出して必要に応じ正しい形に直しましょう。最初の文字がヒントとして示してあります。

1. a dead body that has been preserved by wrapping it in cloth, especially in ancient Egypt

2. a government department that is responsible for one of the areas of government work, such as education or health

3. a way of producing an image of the inside of the human body or a solid object using X-rays or ultrasound

4. the organ inside your head that controls how you think, feel, and move

5. a wound or damage to part of your body caused by an accident or attack

6. a ring of flowers or leaves, worn on your head or around your neck for decoration or for a special ceremony

1. m _____	2. m _____	3. t _____
4. b _____	5. i _____	6. g _____

After reading 3　次の課題について、自分の考えを述べましょう。

あなたが直接触れずに分析したいと思うものは何ですか。またそれを分析したい理由は何ですか。あなたの考えを書いてみましょう。

日本語でのメモ

英語での作文

UNIT 5

NASA aims to make observations from space junk collision with Moon

NASA、月と宇宙ゴミの衝突観測をねらう

宇宙開発の進行に伴い、役割を終えたロケットが宇宙ゴミとして宇宙空間を漂うことが増えています。この Unit では、宇宙ゴミとなった使用済みロケットと月の偶発的な衝突を NASA が観測しようとしていることを報じた記事を取り上げます。

Before reading 1 説明を読み、内容に関する理解を深めましょう。
また図からどんなことが言えるか考えましょう。

出典：外務省ホームページ
(https://www.mofa.go.jp/mofaj/press/pr/wakaru/topics/vol85/index.html)

- 宇宙ゴミ（space junk）は、具体的にはロケットの加速に使われたブースター（booster）です。現在の宇宙技術（space technology）において、ゴミの発生は不可避の宿命（fate）です。月への偶発的な衝突（unintended collision）は今回が初めてとなります。

Before reading 2 日本語に対応する英語表現を選択肢から選び、○で囲みましょう。

1. 天文学者　　　　　astronomer ／ astrogeologist

2. 震度計　　　　　　seismometer ／ sensitometer

3. 小惑星　　　　　　steroid ／ asteroid

4. 弾道、軌道　　　　trailer ／ trajectory

5. 月学、月理学　　　selenology ／ serenology

NASA aims to make observations from space junk collision with Moon

① NASA said Thursday it aims to survey the crater formed when the remains of a SpaceX rocket are expected to crash into the Moon in early March, calling the event an exciting research opportunity.

② The rocket was deployed in 2015 to put a NASA satellite into orbit and its second stage, or booster, has been floating in the cosmos ever since, a common fate for such pieces of space technology.

③ "On its current trajectory, the second stage is expected to impact the far side of the Moon on March 4, 2022," a NASA spokeswoman told AFP.

④ "The impact of the rocket chunk weighing four tons will not be visible from Earth in real time, nor will NASA's Lunar Reconnaissance Orbiter (LRO), which is currently orbiting the Moon, be in a position to observe the impact as it happens," the spokeswoman said.

⑤ The LRO could be used later, however, to capture images for before-and-after comparisons.

⑥ "Finding the crater will be challenging and might take weeks to months," the spokeswoman said, adding that the unique event presents an exciting research opportunity.

⑦ Studying a crater formed by a hurtling object with a known mass and speed (it will be traveling at 9,000 kilometers per hour), as well as the material that the impact stirs up, could help advance selenology, or the scientific study of the moon.

⑧ Spacecraft have been intentionally crashed into the

写真：アフロ

NASA
National Aeronautics and Space Administration
（米国航空宇宙局）の略語

Lunar Reconnaissance Orbiter　月周回衛星

26

Moon before for scientific purposes, such as during the Apollo missions to test seismometers, but this is the first unintended collision to be detected.

⑨ Astronomer Bill Gray, creator of a software used to determine the trajectories of asteroids and other objects, was the first to calculate the booster's new collision course with the Moon.

⑩ He believes that space junk should always be directed towards the moon when possible: "If it hits the moon, then we actually learn something from it," Gray said.

Apollo missions　アポロ計画（NASA の有人による月探査計画）

While reading 1　次に関して、記事を読んで分かったことをメモしてみましょう。

1.　月に衝突する宇宙ゴミについて

....

....

2.　NASA の女性報道官の話

....

....

3.　Bill Gray 氏及び氏の意見について

....

....

column　**Headline の特徴④ 略語、縮約語の使用**

すでに述べたように、Headline では IMF, NATO, IOC, WHO のような略語や、Dept., S'pore といった縮約語が多用されます。縮約語は Dept. や ad. のように語の最後にピリオド (.) がついたり、S'pore や int'l のようにアポストロフィ (') がつくことが多く、読み手はそれらの記号によって縮約語であると知ることができます。しかし記事によっては dept や intl のように、そのような記号さえも省略されることがあります。

Task　次の４つの記事の Headline で縮約されている部分を○で囲み、元の形を書いてみましょう。

(1) U.N. says world eating too much sugar
(2) Dalai Lama calls for intl investigation
(3) 'Low-cost airfare era' to begin this yr?
(4) Govt to set target for '50 emissions

While reading 2　記事の中で次の情報が述べられている段落の番号を書きましょう。

1. 月に衝突するロケットが打ち上げられた年：[　　　]
2. ロケットが月に衝突する日：[　　　]
3. 宇宙を移動する物体の速度：[　　　]
4. 小惑星等の軌道を計算するソフトを作った天文学者の名前：[　　　]

While reading 3　空欄に適切な単語または数字を入れ、記事の要約を完成させましょう。
答えが単語の場合、最初の文字がヒントとして示してあります。

On January 27, 2022, NASA said it aims to survey the crater formed when the ¹⁾r_____ of a SpaceX rocket are expected to crash into the far side of the Moon on March 4, 2022. The rocket was deployed in ²⁾_____ to put a NASA satellite into orbit and its second stage has been ³⁾f_____ in the cosmos ever since. According to a NASA spokeswoman, the impact of the rocket chunk weighing four tons will not be ⁴⁾v_____ from Earth in real time, and finding the crater will be challenging and might take weeks to months. She added that the unique event presents an exciting research ⁵⁾o_____.

While reading 4　3で空欄に入れた単語または数字が正しいか、音声で確認しましょう。

🔊 1-32

While reading 5　記事が示唆する内容と合致すれば T、しなければ F を記入しましょう。

1. The second stage of a SpaceX rocket has been floating in the cosmos for more than 10 years.　[　　　]

2. The crater of the impact will be found in early March.　[　　　]

3. NASA had never detected an unintended crash of a spacecraft into the Moon before January 2022.　[　　　]

4. Nobody had calculated the booster's new collision course with the Moon before astronomer Bill Gray did.　[　　　]

 **After reading 1** 語句を並べ替えて英文を完成させましょう。間違った場合、解答欄に正しい答えを書くこと。なお文頭に来る語句も小文字にしてあります。

1. 天文学者のビル・グレイ氏は月とブースターの新たな衝突の航路を計算した最初の人だった。

Astronomer Bill Gray (to / was / with / calculate / the first / the booster's new collision course) the Moon.

予想 : ....

解答 : *Astronomer Bill Gray* ....
.... *the Moon.*

2. そのロケットはそれ以来宇宙をさまよっている。

(in / has / been / floating / the cosmos / the rocket) ever since.

予想 : ....

解答 : .... *ever since.*

3. ロケットの塊の衝撃はリアルタイムでは地球から見えないだろう。

The impact of the rocket chunk (be / not / from / will / Earth / visible) in real time.

予想 : ....

解答 : *The impact of the rocket chunk* ....
.... *in real time.*

4. 報道官の女性はクレーターを見つけるのに数週間から数ヶ月はかかるかもしれないと述べた。

The spokeswoman said (to / take / might / weeks / months / finding the crater).

予想 : ....

解答 : *The spokeswoman said* ....
....

 **After reading 2** 次の説明はどの語についてのものか、文中から抜き出して必要に応じ正しい形に直しましょう。最初の文字がヒントとして示してあります。

1. a round hole in the ground made by something that has fallen on it or by an explosion

2. a machine that has been sent into space and goes around the Earth, Moon, etc., used for radio, television, and other electronic communication

3. to move slowly on water or in the air

4. to move very fast in a particular direction

5. a large amount of a substance which does not have a definite or regular shape

6. old or unwanted objects that have no use or value

1. c _____	2. s _____	3. f _____
4. h _____	5. m _____	6. j _____

After reading 3 次の課題について、自分の考えを述べましょう。

宇宙や深海などで観測してみたいと思うものは何ですか。またそう思う理由は何ですか。あなたの考えを書いてみましょう。

日本語でのメモ

英語での作文

UNIT 6

Hospitals to get guidelines against ransomware attacks

病院、ランサムウェア攻撃に対する指針を得る見通し

近年、世界各地で重要インフラがサイバー攻撃の被害を受ける事態が起きています。この Unit では、国内の病院へのランサムウェア攻撃に対する指針を厚生労働省が策定することを報じた記事を取り上げます。

Before reading 1 説明を読み、内容に関する理解を深めましょう。
また図からどんなことが言えるか考えましょう。

-ランサムウェア (ransomware) によるサイバー攻撃 (cyber-attack) でコンピューターがウイルス (virus) に感染 (infection) すると、中のデータは暗号化され、電子カルテ (electronic chart) 等が閲覧できなくなります。

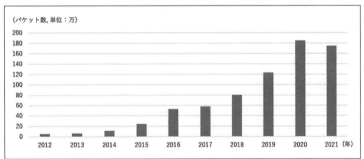

図1 IP アドレス当たりの年間総観測パケット数（過去 10 年間）

(パケット数, 単位：万)

出典：情報通信研究機構 NICTER 観測レポート 2021 より

Before reading 2 日本語に対応する英語表現を選択肢から選び、〇で囲みましょう。

1.	メール送信者	email sender / email recipient
2.	添付ファイル	attached file / attended file
3.	草案、原案	draft plan / viable plan
4.	医療機関	medical instigate / medical institution
5.	厚生労働省	the Health, Labor and Welfare Ministry / the Health, Welfare and Labor Ministry

Hospitals to get guidelines against ransomware attacks

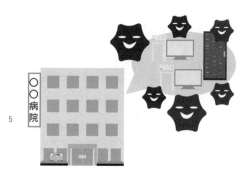

① Following a spate of ransomware attacks targeting medical institutions, the Health, Labor and Welfare Ministry will compile information security guidelines designed for hospitals within fiscal 2021, which ends on March 31, 2022.

② The guidelines will state that backup data, such as electronic medical records, should be kept separately from hospital networks in order to limit damage.

③ According to ministry sources, backup data could be infected with ransomware and become inaccessible if it is connected online to the hospital's system. The ministry therefore will ask hospitals to save their backup data in a separate system, and also to specify the type of media to be used for saving it and the frequency of updates.

④ Infection of backup data could cause long-term problems. Tsurugi municipal Handa Hospital in Tokushima Prefecture, for example, suffered a cyber-attack on its backup data at the end of October, and it was estimated to take a couple of months for the hospital to resume treatment as normal in the wake of the incident.

⑤ Under the guidelines, email senders are urged not to attach any files but instead to text the content via a message board, because viruses can be embedded in attached files. The guideline will ask hospitals to introduce anti-ransomware software and conduct cyber-attack drills.

⑥ In 2005, the ministry drew up guidelines on information

写真：イメージマート

a spate of ～　大量の～

Tsurugi municipal
Handa Hospital
つるぎ町立半田病院

in the wake of ～
～の結果として

anti-ransomware
software ランサムウェア
対策ソフト
cyber-attack drill
サイバー攻撃を想定した訓練
draw up ～
～を作成する

security in response to extensive use of electronic charts, and urged medical institutions to deploy a cybersecurity officer. These existing guidelines, however, are about 160 pages long, and the ministry plans to condense the
35 contents and make it easier to understand. Its draft plan will be drawn up this month to undergo a public comment session in February before being officially issued.

⑦ A man who heads the Tokyo-based Medical Information System Development Center and also is in charge of the
40 team compiling the new guidelines, said "We must create effective guidelines that can be understood and utilized easily to cope with the rampant cyber-attacks on medical institutions."

Medical Information System Development Center 一般財団法人 医療情報システム開発センター

⊛ *While reading* 1

次に関して、記事を読んで分かったことをメモしてみましょう。

1. ランサムウェア攻撃による被害

....

....

2. 2005 年に作成されたガイドライン

....

....

3. 新ガイドラインに盛り込まれる内容

....

....

▤ column ┃ Headline の特徴⑤つづりの短い語の使用

同じような意味を表わす語が 2 つ以上ある場合、Headline ではつづりの短い方を用います。例えば「援助する」の意味を表わす語には aid や assist、「問題」には issue や problem などの語がありますが、新聞英語では特別な事情がない限り短い方の aid や issue が使用されます。

Task 次の 3 つの Headline で使われている単語のうち、新聞英語に特徴的なものを○で囲んでみましょう。

(1) White hackers eyed for cyberdefense
(2) Obama moves to tighten gun control
(3) France moves to ban ultrathin models

1. 2021 年度が終了する日：[　　　]

2. つるぎ町立半田病院がある都道府県：[　　　]

3. ガイドラインでメール送信者に求められていること：[　　　]

4. 2005 年に作成されたガイドラインのページ数：[　　　]

While reading 3　空欄に適切な単語または数字を入れ、記事の要約を完成させましょう。答えが単語の場合、最初の文字がヒントとして示してあります。

In response to extensive use of electronic ¹⁾c＿＿＿＿＿＿, the Health, Labor and Welfare Ministry drew up guidelines on information security in ²⁾＿＿＿＿, and urged medical institutions to deploy a cybersecurity officer. Nevertheless, there were a spate of ransomware ³⁾a＿＿＿＿＿ targeting medical institutions. The ministry thus will compile information security guidelines designed for hospitals within fiscal 2021. The guidelines will state that ⁴⁾b＿＿＿＿＿ data, such as electronic medical records, should be kept separately from hospital networks in order to limit ⁵⁾d＿＿＿＿＿.

While reading 4　3 で空欄に入れた単語または数字が正しいか、音声で確認しましょう。

🔊 1-37

While reading 5　記事が示唆する内容と合致すれば T、しなければ F を記入しましょう。

1. Tsurugi municipal Handa Hospital provided treatment as normal in November, 2021.　[　　　]

2. Texting the content via a message board has a smaller risk of infection than using attached files.　[　　　]

3. Electronic charts were not widely used in Japan in the late 2000s.　[　　　]

4. New guidelines to be compiled within fiscal 2021 will have more than 180 pages.　[　　　]

 **After reading 1**　語句を並べ替えて英文を完成させましょう。間違った場合、解答欄に正しい答えを書くこと。

1. バックアップデータは病院のシステムにオンラインでつながると接続不能になる可能性がある。

Backup data could (if / is / it / become / connected / inaccessible) to the hospital's system.

予想： ....

解答： *Backup data could*
　　　　　　　to the hospital's system.

2. 電子メールの送信者は内容を本文に書き込むよう促される。

Email senders (to / are / via / text / urged / the content) a message board.

予想： ....

解答： *Email senders*
　　　　a message board.

3. その省は内容をわかりやすくすることを計画している。

The ministry (to / to / make / plans / easier / the contents) understand.

予想： ....

解答： *The ministry*
　　　　　　understand.

4. その人物は新ガイドラインの策定作業を行うチームを統括している。

The person (in / is / of / charge / compiling / the team) the new guidelines.

予想： ....

解答： *The person*
　　　　the new guidelines.

 **After reading 2** 次の説明はどの語についてのものか、文中から抜き出して必要に応じ正しい形に直しましょう。最初の文字がヒントとして示してあります。

1. something that you can use to replace something that does not work or is lost

2. to state something in an exact and detailed way

3. the number of times that something happens within a particular period of time or within a particular group of people

4. to start doing something again after stopping or being interrupted

5. to make something that is spoken or written shorter, by not giving as much detail or using fewer words to give the same information

6. to experience something, especially a change or something unpleasant

1. b _____	2. s _____	3. f _____
4. r _____	5. c _____	6. u _____

After reading 3 次の課題について、自分の考えを述べましょう。

あなたはサイバー攻撃から自分のパソコンを保護するためにどんなことをしていますか。またこれからどんなことをしていきたいですか。あなたの考えを書いてみましょう。

UNIT 7

NFT museum opens its doors in United States

米国で NFT に特化した美術館が開館

 普通のデジタルデータは複製されると出所がわからなくなりますが、近年、所有権を記録できるデジタルデータが作られています。この Unit では、この技術を用いて作成されたデジタルアート作品のみを扱った美術館が開館したことを報じた記事を取り上げます。

🔲 Before reading 1

説明を読み、内容に関する理解を深めましょう。
また図からどんなことが言えるか考えましょう。

-NFT とは「非代替性トークン」(Non-Fungible Token) の略称で、ブロックチェーン (blockchain) 技術を活用しています。

-NFT は、大量の (innumerable) 複製が可能 (copyable) な一方、オリジナルに所有権 (ownership) を与える (confer) ことができるという特徴を持っています。

ブロックチェーン技術による社会変革の可能性

* 記載金額は、ブロックチェーン技術が影響を及ぼす可能性のある市場規模

1. **価値の流通・ポイント化、プラットフォームのインフラ化**
   自治体等が発行する地域通貨を、ブロックチェーンで流通・管理
   地域通貨 | 電子クーポン | ポイントサービス | 市場規模 1 兆円

2. **権利証明行為の非中央集権化の実現**
   土地の物理的呪況や権利関係の情報を、ブロックチェーン上で登録・公示・管理
   土地登記 | 電子カルテ | 各種登録 (出生・婚姻・転居) | 市場規模 1 兆円

3. **遊休資産ゼロ・高効率シェアリングの実現**
   資産等の利用権移転情報、提供者／利用者の評価情報をブロックチェーン上に記録
   デジタルコンテンツ | チケットサービス | C2C オークション | 市場規模 13 兆円

4. **オープン・高効率なサプライチェーンの実現**
   製品の原材料からの製造過程と流通・販売までを、ブロックチェーン上で追跡
   小売り | 貴金属管理 | 美術品等真贋認証 | 市場規模 32 兆円

5. **プロセス・取引の全自動化・効率化の実現**
   契約条件、履行内容、将来発生するプロセス等を、ブロックチェーン上に記録
   遺言 | IoT | 電力サービス | 市場規模 20 兆円

出典：「ブロックチェーン技術を利用したサービスに関する国内外動向調査」(総務省)
(https://www.meti.go.jp/main/infographic/pdf/block_c.pdf) をもとに作成

🔲 Before reading 2

日本語に対応する英語表現を選択肢から選び、○で囲みましょう。

1. 収集家　　　　　　　collector / corrector

2. 熱狂　　　　　　　　craze / braze

3. 共同創設者　　　　　co-founder / confounder

4. 暗号通貨、仮想通貨　cryptocurrency / crystal currency

5. 世界的現象　　　　　global phenolic / global phenomenon

NFT museum opens its doors in United States

写真：AFP/WAA

① A museum dedicated to NFTs—the blockchain-based creations that have taken the artworld by storm—has opened its doors in the United States.

② The Seattle NFT Museum features original artworks along with explanations of the technology behind them, and is intended to help visitors navigate the new world of Non-Fungible Tokens.

③ "The point of a physical space is to make it easier for anyone to access," museum co-founder Peter Hamilton told AFP.

④ "You can walk in here, and depending on how much you know or don't know about digital art, about NFTs, it doesn't really matter, because you can see the art in a large format display, in a way that would remind you, or be familiar, of a museum exhibition."

⑤ NFTs are unique digital objects that confer ownership.

⑥ While their content may be copyable, the NFT is the original, in much the same way that there are innumerable prints of Leonardo da Vinci's Mona Lisa, but only the Louvre museum has the original.

⑦ Investors and wealthy collectors have clamored in recent months to get involved in the latest digital craze, which relies on the same blockchain technology that powers cryptocurrencies.

⑧ Recent auctions have seen eye-watering sums paid for

take ~ by storm
〜をとりこにする

a large format display
大型（大画面）の展示

Leonardo da Vinci
レオナルド・ダ・ビンチ
（イタリアの美術家、科学者）
Mona Lisa
「モナリザ」（ルーブル美術館にあるレオナルド・ダ・ビンチの絵画作品）

NFTs, including $69.3 million for a digital work by artist Beeple at a sale at Christie's.

⑨ Like all new technologies, they have their doubters; some observers dismiss them as a fad, or worse—something akin
35 to the Emperor's New Clothes.

⑩ But visitors to the museum said they sensed something real.

⑪ "It's kind of a global phenomenon so we're kind of watching it come to life," said one museum guest, who
40 gave her name as Cara.

⑫ Watching that evolution is all part of the fun for Hamilton.

⑬ "It's hard to say where this technology is going to lead us, this is really just the beginning," he said.

45 ⑭ "Anyone that tells you they're an NFT expert is not telling you the truth because we are all learning, we are all starting from a very very early experience."

Christie's ロンドンの美術品競売商

akin to 〜 〜に似ている

Emperor's New Clothes 高評価の物事を批判するのをためらうこと（アンデルセンの同名童話『裸の王様』より）

 While reading 1 次に関して、記事を読んで分かったことをメモしてみましょう。

1. NFT について

....

2. NFT 美術館について

....

☰ column　**Headline の特徴⑥ 簡潔な表現の問題点**

すでに述べたように、Headline ではメッセージの意味・内容と大きく関連しない機能語（例：特別動詞や接続詞）を省略したり、省スペースの表現（例：縮約語やつづりの短い語）を多用するなど、メッセージを効率的に示すための工夫をしています。他方で、機能語の省略や省スペース表現の多用はいろいろな解釈を可能にしてしまうという問題を伴います。例えば新聞英語の現在形は過去形と現在完了の両方の解釈ができます。また Rep. という縮約語は Republican（[米国の] 共和党員）にも Representative（[米国の] 下院議員）にも解釈することができます。こういった場合の判断には Headline 全体あるいはその先の Lead や Body まで読むことが重要です。

Task　次の 2 つの Headline にある Gov という語はそれぞれ何を縮約したものか考えてみましょう。

(1) German <u>Gov</u>. spies on citizens
(2) Lawyer to challenge <u>Gov</u>. Clinton in Arkansas

記事の中で次の情報が述べられている段落の番号を書きましょう。

1. NFT 美術館のある都市の名前：[　　　]

2. ピーター・ハミルトン氏の地位：[　　　]

3. 「モナリザ」を所有する美術館の名前：[　　　]

4. 6930 万ドルで落札された作品の制作者の名前：[　　　]

While reading 3　空欄に適切な単語を入れ、記事の要約を完成させましょう。
最初の文字がヒントとして示してあります。

NFTs are unique digital objects that confer 1)o＿＿＿＿＿＿＿ and rely on the same blockchain technology that powers cryptocurrencies. Investors and wealthy 2)c＿＿＿＿＿＿＿ have clamored in recent months to get involved in the latest digital craze, and recent 3)a＿＿＿＿＿＿＿ have seen eye-watering sums paid for NFTs. Under such circumstances, a museum dedicated to NFTs has opened its doors in the United States. The Seattle NFT Museum features 4)o＿＿＿＿＿＿＿ artworks along with explanations of the technology behind them, and is intended to help visitors navigate the new world of Non-Fungible 5)T＿＿＿＿＿＿＿.

While reading 4　3で空欄に入れた単語が正しいか、音声で確認しましょう。

🔊 1-45

While reading 5　記事が示唆する内容と合致すれば T、しなければ F を記入しましょう。

1. The NFT Museum in Seattle exhibits traditional artworks as well as those using the blockchain technology.　[　　　]

2. According to Hamilton, people can enjoy artworks at the museum even if they have little knowledge about NFTs.　[　　　]

3. The technology used for cryptocurrencies is basically different from that used for NFTs.　[　　　]

4. According to Hamilton, those who call themselves NFT experts may not know everything about NFTs.　[　　　]

 **After reading 1** 　語句を並べ替えて英文を完成させましょう。間違った場合、解答欄に
正しい答えを書くこと。

1. NFT に特化した美術館が米国で開館した。

A museum (to / has / NFTs / opened / dedicated / its doors) in the United States.

予想： ....

....

解答： *A museum*

　　　　　　　　　　　in the United States.

2. その要点は誰もがより容易にアクセスできるようにすることだ。

The point (is / it / to / for / make / easier) anyone to access.

予想： ....

解答： *The point* 　　　　　　　　　　　　　　　　*anyone to access.*

3. その美術館には訪問者の非代替性トークンの新しい世界での航海を支援するねらい
がある。

The museum (is / to / help / intended / navigate / visitors) the new world of Non-Fungible Tokens.

予想： ....

....

解答： *The museum*

　　　　the new world of Non-Fungible Tokens.

4. 投資家は最新のデジタルの流行に関わろうと騒ぎ立てている。

Investors have (in / to / get / clamored / involved / the recent digital craze).

予想： ....

....

解答： *Investors have*

....

 **After reading 2** 次の説明はどの語についてのものか、文中から抜き出して必要に応じ正しい形に直しましょう。最初の文字がヒントとして示してあります。

1. to use a place, time, money, etc., only for a particular purpose

2. a building where important cultural, historical, or scientific objects are kept and shown to the public

3. to officially give someone a title, etc., especially as a reward for something they have achieved

4. someone who gives money to a company, business, or bank in order to get a profit

5. a public meeting where land, buildings, paintings, etc., are sold to the person who offers the most money for them

6. something that people like or do for a short time, or that is fashionable for a short time

1. d _____	2. m _____	3. c _____
4. i _____	5. a _____	6. f _____

After reading 3 次の課題について、自分の考えを述べましょう。

もし日本に非代替性トークンに特化した美術館が誕生したら、そこに行ってみたいと思いますか。またそう思う／思わない理由は何ですか。あなたの考えを書いてみましょう。

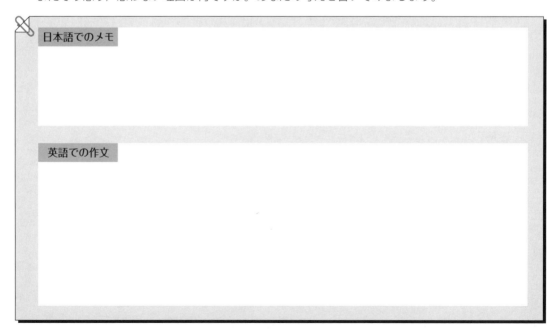

日本語でのメモ

英語での作文

Tiger breeding, exports flourish in S. Africa — charity

トラの繁殖、輸出が南アフリカで盛んに——愛護団体が警告

動物園で人気の動物の一つであるトラ。みなさんはトラの個体数が減少しつつあることを知っていますか？ この Unit では、南アフリカで繁殖させたトラを輸出するビジネスが広がっていることを報じた記事を取り上げます。

📥 Before reading 1

説明を読み、内容に関する理解を深めましょう。
また図からどんなことが言えるか考えましょう。

- 世界におけるトラの個体数 (population) は 100 年近くの間に大幅に減少（decline）しており、絶滅危惧種（threatened species）に指定されています。

- 南アフリカ（South Africa）ではトラの個体数に関する正式統計（official count）は取られていません。また大型ネコ科の商業繁殖（commercial breeding）は違法にはなっていません。

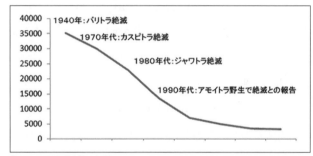

急減する野生トラの生息数

1940年：バリトラ絶滅
1970年代：カスピトラ絶滅
1980年代：ジャワトラ絶滅
1990年代：アモイトラ野生で絶滅との報告

Source: World Bank Group

📥 Before reading 2

日本語に対応する英語表現を選択肢から選び、○で囲みましょう。

1. 商業狩猟　　　　　　commercial hunting ／ commercial haunting

2. 動物愛護団体　　　　animal welfare group ／ animal workfare group

3. 法的保護　　　　　　legal protection ／ lawyer protection

4. 国内法　　　　　　　national legislation ／ national registration

5. 抜け穴　　　　　　　foxhole ／ loophole

Tiger breeding, exports flourish in S. Africa—charity

① South Africa's legal lion breeding has spawned a tiger farming industry for commercial exports, potentially posing a threat to the species

写真：AFP/WAA

commercial export
商業輸出

already in decline, an animal welfare group warned Tuesday.

② Breeding lions for commercial hunting and for bone exports towards Asia is legal in South Africa, but in recent years tiger breeding for similar purposes has become more common.

③ A report by global animal rights charity, Four Paws, showed that 359 tigers—almost a tenth of the global tiger population—were exported from South Africa from 2011-2020.

④ Around 255 of them were sold to zoos.

⑤ Tigers are not native to South Africa and enjoy no legal protection in the country, the organisation said.

⑥ There were loopholes that were allowing the business model to change, Paws's wildlife expert Kieran Harkin told AFP.

wildlife expert
野生生物専門家

⑦ "The market being in Asia was already there, demand was there, so it made perfect sense for the (breeders) to move over to the tiger, which was again even more lucrative than lions," he said.

⑧ South Africa has no official count of its tiger population.

⑨ Four Paws is asking South Africa to halt the commercial breeding of all big cats, whose populations are declining partly due to trade to Asian countries.

all big cats
すべての大型ネコ科動物

44

⑩ "We are asking South Africa to stop supporting that trade... and be a defender of the wildlife, and not perpetuating the trade in species on the decline," Harkin said in an online interview from London.

35 ⑪ He accused South Africa of flouting international laws that dictate that tigers should not be bred for trade in their parts.

⑫ South Africa's government promised to give a comment later on Tuesday.

40 ⑬ "As the largest exporter of big cat parts, South Africa is being urged to reverse that role and take on a leading position in protecting wildlife... iconic species," Harkin said.

take on ～ ～を引き受ける

⑭ Fiona Miles, director of Four Paws in South Africa,
45 called for national legislation and international agreements to be re-examined since they are clearly not working.

call for ～ ～を要求する

⑮ She warned in a statement that unless the threatened species were protected, we put all big cat species at risk of one day, only existing behind bars.

put ～ at risk
～を危険にさらす

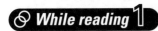 **While reading 1**　次に関して、記事を読んで分かったことをメモしてみましょう。

1.　南アフリカの大型ネコ科動物に対する法的保護

....

2.　Harkin 氏の発言

....

> 📃 **column**　**Lead の特徴**
>
> 記事全文のうち最初の部分を Lead（前文）と言います。Lead は記事の書き出しであると同時に記事全文の要約でもあります。Lead には「5W1H」、つまり Who, What, When, Where, Why, How（誰が、何を、いつ、どこで、なぜ、どのように）に関する情報が簡潔に含まれていて、この部分を読むだけで記事の要旨が理解できます。Lead は読み手、特に記事に最後まで目を通す時間のない人にとって大切な役割を担っています。
>
> **Task**　Unit 6 (Hospitals to get guidelines against ransomware attacks) の Lead（第一段落）を読み、5W1H のうちどの情報が含まれているかを確認しましょう。

1. 動物愛護団体が報告を行った曜日：[　　　　]

2. 2011 年〜 2020 年の間に南アフリカから輸出されたトラの頭数：[　　　　]

3. Harkin 氏に取材を行った通信社の名前：[　　　　]

4. Fiona Miles 氏の地位：[　　　　]

Breeding lions for commercial hunting and for bone exports towards Asia is
1)l_____ in South Africa, but in recent years tiger breeding for
similar purposes has become more common. A report by global animal rights
2)c_____, Four Paws, showed that 359 tigers were exported from South
Africa from 2011-2020. Around 3)_____ of them were sold to zoos. Four Paws
is asking South Africa to halt the commercial breeding of all big cats, whose
4)p_____ are declining partly due to trade to Asian countries. South
Africa's government promised to give a 5)c_____ later on February 1,
2022.

🔊 1-54

1. Breeding lions for commercial hunting is against the law in South Africa.
[　　　　]

2. There are fewer than 5,000 tigers in the world.　[　　　　]

3. More than half of the tigers exported from South Africa between 2011 and
2020 were sold to zoos.　[　　　　]

4. According to Harkin, the market in Asia wants to buy tigers from South
Africa.　[　　　　]

 語句を並べ替えて英文を完成させましょう。間違った場合、解答欄に正しい答えを書くこと。

1. アジアに骨を輸出する目的でライオンを繁殖させることは南アフリカでは合法である。

Breeding lions (is / for / Asia / legal / towards / bone exports) in South Africa.

予想： ....

解答： *Breeding lions* ....
.... *in South Africa.*

2. 南アフリカは野生生物の保護に関して主導的な役割を担うよう促されている。

South Africa is (on / to / take / being / urged / a leading position) in protecting wildlife.

予想： ....

解答： *South Africa is* ....
.... *in protecting wildlife.*

3. マイルズさんは国内法が機能していないのが明確であるため再検討を要求した。

Miles (be / to / for / called / national legislation / re-examined) since it is clearly not working.

予想： ....

解答： *Miles* ....
.... *since it is clearly not working.*

4. 我々は南アフリカが野生生物の守護者になるようお願いしている。

We (be / to / are / asking / South Africa / a defender) of wildlife.

予想： ....

解答： *We* ....
of wildlife.

 **After reading 2** 次の説明はどの語についてのものか、文中から抜き出して必要に応じ正しい形に直しましょう。最初の文字がヒントとして示してあります。

1. a decrease in the quality, quantity, or importance of something

2. to keep animals or plants in order to produce babies or new plants, especially ones with particular qualities

3. a small mistake in a law that makes it possible to avoid doing something that the law is supposed to make you do

4. the need or desire that people have for particular goods and services

5. producing a large amount of money; making a large profit

6. to make a situation, attitude, etc., especially a bad one, continue to exist for a long time

1. d _____	2. b _____	3. l _____
4. d _____	5. l _____	6. p _____

 **After reading 3** 次の課題について、自分の考えを述べましょう。

トラの絶滅を防ぐために、どのような取り組みが必要だと思いますか。またその取り組みが必要だと思う理由は何ですか。あなたの考えを書いてみましょう。

日本語でのメモ

英語での作文

UNIT 9

Spring in February — UK plants flowering 'a month early'

2月の春──英国の植物、1月早く開花

みなさんは地球温暖化の影響を感じることはありますか。もし感じる場合、それはどんな時ですか。この Unit では、温暖化の影響で英国の植物がこれまでより1月早く開花したことを報じた記事を取り上げます。

🔲 **Before reading 1**　説明を読み、内容に関する理解を深めましょう。
また図からどんなことが言えるか考えましょう。

- 植物 (plant) の種類には、高木 (tree)、低木 (shrub)、草本 (herb)、ツル性植物 (climbing plant) などがあります。

- 開花時期の早期化 (early flowing) は、人間が引き起こした気候変動 (human-caused climate change) の影響の加速 (accelerating impact) と一致する (coincide) ようです。

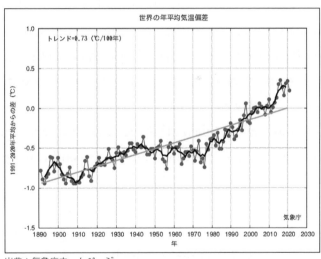

出典：気象庁ホームページ
(https://www.data.jma.go.jp/cpdinfo/temp/an_wld.html)

🔲 **Before reading 2**　日本語に対応する英語表現を選択肢から選び、○で囲みましょう。

1. 気温、温度　　　　　tempelature / temperature

2. アマチュア　　　　　amature / amateur

3. 庭師　　　　　　　　gardener / gardenist

4. 博物学者　　　　　　naturer / naturalist

5. 英国王立気象学会　　Loyal Meteorological Society /
　　　　　　　　　　　Royal Meteorological Society

49

Spring in February
— UK plants flowering 'a month early'

① Global warming is causing plants in the UK to burst into flower around a month earlier, with potentially profound consequences for crops and wildlife, according to research Wednesday that used nature observations going back to the 1700s.

② Trees, herbs and other flowering plants have shifted seasonal rhythms as temperatures have increased, according to the study led by the University of Cambridge.

③ "The results are truly alarming because of the ecological threats posed by early flowering," said Ulf Buntgen, a professor from Cambridge's Department of Geography, who led the research published in the journal Proceedings of the Royal Society B.

④ Crops can be killed off if they blossom early and are then lashed by a late frost, but researchers said the bigger threat was to wildlife.

⑤ This is because insects and birds have evolved to synchronize their own development stages with the plants they rely on. When they are no longer in phase, the result is an ecological mismatch.

⑥ "A certain plant flowers, it attracts a particular type of insect, which attracts a particular type of bird, and so on," Buntgen said in a press release from the university.

⑦ "But if one component responds faster than the others, there's a risk that they'll be out of synch, which can lead species to collapse if they can't adapt quickly enough."

写真 : Science Photo Library / アフロ

burst into 〜
突然〜する

University of Cambridge
ケンブリッジ大学

Ulf Buntgen
ウルフ・ビュントゲン氏
Department of Geography　地理学科
Proceedings of the Royal Society B
英国王立協会紀要 B

kill off 〜　〜を全滅させる

late frost　遅霜
(晩春になって降りる霜で、作物に害を与える)

no longer 〜
もはや〜ない
in phase
一致して、同調して

press release　公式発表

out of synch
調子などがずれて、同調しないで

50

Spring backwards?

⑧ To track the changes in flowering patterns, researchers used a database known as Nature's Calendar, which has entries by scientists, naturalists, amateur and professional gardeners, as well as organizations such as the Royal Meteorological Society, going back more than 200 years.

⑨ Looking at more than 400,000 observations of 406 trees, shrubs, herbs and climbing plants across swathes of Britain, they found that the average first flowering date from 1987 to 2019 is 30 days earlier than the average first flowering date from 1753 to 1986.

⑩ The changes seen in recent decades coincide with accelerating impacts of human-caused climate change, especially higher temperatures.

⑪ "Spring in Britain might eventually creep into the historically wintry month of February if global temperatures continue to increase at their current rate," said Buntgen.

creep into ～
～にそっと入り込む

⑫ "That rapid shift in natural cycles could reverberate through forests, farms and gardens."

reverberate　反響する

≡ column　| **Body の特徴**

記事全文のうち Lead を除く部分を Body（本文）と言います。Body は通常複数の段落から構成され、Headline や Lead で示された要点を詳しく説明する役割を担っています。Body の段落は情報の核心部分（＝重要度が高い部分）から順に配列され、段落が下がるに従って補足的、周辺的（＝重要度が低い）になっていきます。このような段落構成を「逆三角形型」または「逆ピラミッド型」（inverted pyramid style）と呼びますが、この構成は読み手にとって情報を効率的に把握できるメリットが、書き手にとっては記事の量を調節する際に書き直す手間が省けるメリットがあります。

情報の核心部分
↓
周辺・補足部分

Task　Unit 6 (Hospitals to get guidelines against raosomeware attacks) の Body（第2段落～第7段落）を読み、各段落でどのような情報が含まれているか確認してみましょう。

⊗ While reading 1 次に関して、記事を読んで分かったことをメモしてみましょう。

ビュントゲン教授の発言

....

⊗ While reading 2 記事の中で次の情報が述べられている段落の番号を書きましょう。

1. 研究の結果が発表された曜日： [　　　　]

2. 研究が掲載された学術誌の名前： [　　　　]

3. Nature's Calendar に情報を提供している組織の名前： [　　　　]

4. 研究チームが調査した植物の種類の数： [　　　　]

⊗ While reading 3 空欄に適切な単語または数字を入れ、記事の要約を完成させましょう。答えが単語の場合、最初の文字がヒントとして示してあります。

Global warming is causing plants in the UK to burst into [1)]f_____ around a month earlier, with potentially profound consequences for crops and wildlife, according to research that used nature observations going back to the [2)]_____s. Crops can be killed off if they blossom early and are then lashed by a late [3)]f_____, but researchers said the bigger threat was to wildlife. This is because [4)]i_____ and birds have evolved to synchronize their own development stages with the plants they rely on. When they are no longer in phase, the result is an ecological [5)]m_____.

⊗ While reading 4 3で空欄に入れた単語または数字が正しいか、音声で確認しましょう。

🔊 1-61

⊗ While reading 5 記事が示唆する内容と合致すれば T、しなければ F を記入しましょう。

1. According to researchers, wildlife will be more affected than crops by early flowering.　[　　　　]

2. The Royal Meteorological Society has been providing information to a database known as Nature's Calendar.　[　　　　]

3. Nature's Calendar was started in the late 19th century.　[　　　　]

4. The average first flowering date in the 19th century was at the beginning of March.　[　　　　]

語句を並べ替えて英文を完成させましょう。間違った場合、解答欄に正しい答えを書くこと。なお文頭に来る語句も小文字にしてあります。

1. 教授はそのジャーナルに掲載された研究を主導した。

(in / led / published / the journal / the research / the professor).

予 想 : ....

解 答 : ....

2. 昆虫は依存する植物の成長段階に同期しようと進化してきた。

Insects have (to / with / evolved / synchronize / the plants / their own development stages) they rely on.

予 想 : ....

....

解 答 : *Insects have*

they rely on.

3. 地球温暖化によって、植物は約1月早く花が咲くようになってきている。

Global warming (is / to / into / burst / plants / causing) flower around a month earlier.

予 想 : ....

....

解 答 : *Global warming*

flower around a month earlier.

4. そのリスクは、（生物）種が迅速に適応できない場合、絶滅につながる可能性がある。

The risk (if / to / can / lead / species / collapse) they can't adapt quickly enough.

予 想 : ....

....

解 答 : *The risk* *they*

can't adapt quickly enough.

 **After reading 2** 次の説明はどの語についてのものか、文中から抜き出して必要に応じ正しい形に直しましょう。最初の文字がヒントとして示してあります。

1. a plant such as wheat, rice, or fruit that is grown by farmers and used as food

2. a small plant that is used to improve the taste of food, or to make medicine

3. a small creature such as a fly or ant, that has six legs, and sometimes wings

4. to happen at exactly the same time, or to arrange for two or more actions to happen at exactly the same time

5. a combination of things or people that do not work well together or are not suitable for each other

6. to gradually change your behavior and attitudes in order to be successful in a new situation

1. c _____	2. h _____	3. i _____
4. s _____	5. m _____	6. a _____

 **After reading 3** 次の課題について、自分の考えを述べましょう。

あなたは地球温暖化を止めることは可能だと思いますか、それとも不可能だと思いますか。またそう思う理由は何ですか。あなたの考えを書いてみましょう。

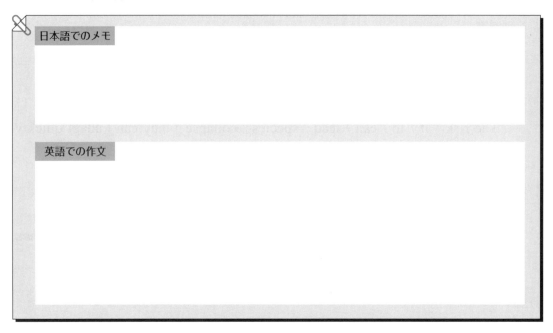

日本語でのメモ

英語での作文

UNIT 10

Japan, U.S. mulling tech export controls

日米、技術の輸出制限を検討中

近年、中国が政治、経済、軍事の多方面で国際的な存在感を高めています。この **Unit** では、民間の先端技術を活用して軍事力を高める同国への警戒から、日本と米国が先端技術の輸出制限を検討していることを報じた記事を取り上げます。

🔲 Before reading 1

説明を読み、内容に関する理解を深めましょう。
また図からどんなことが言えるか考えましょう。

- 軍事力（military power）の強化と関連がある先端技術（advanced technology）の輸出規制（export controls）を行う多国間の枠組み（multilateral framework）は、東西冷戦時代初期の 1949 年に西側諸国（Western nations）が設立した対共産圏輸出統制委員会（Coordinating Committee for Multilateral Export Controls）を想起させます。

日本・中国・アメリカのGDPの推移

(100万米ドル)

総務省統計局資料より作成

🔲 Before reading 2

日本語に対応する英語表現を選択肢から選び、○で囲みましょう。

1. オランダ　　　　　　　the Howland / the Netherlands
2. 民間部門　　　　　　　public sector / private-sector
3. 人工知能　　　　　　　artistic intelligence / artificial intelligence
4. 半導体　　　　　　　　semiconductor / lighting conductor
5. 量子暗号　　　　　　　quantum cryptography / qualifier cryptography

Japan, U.S. mulling tech export controls

① The Japanese and U.S. governments are considering the creation of a multilateral framework to regulate the export of advanced technology, according to several sources. Japan and the United States want to cooperate with like-minded countries in Europe and block exports of such technology to China, which seeks to utilize private-sector technology to boost its military capabilities.

② They are currently specifying the fields to be subject to regulation, which would likely include semiconductor manufacturing equipment, quantum cryptography and artificial intelligence.

③ In a separate framework, the administration of U.S. President Joe Biden has already announced that the United States, along with several other countries, will regulate technology that could contribute to human rights abuses.

④ Japan and the United States are concerned that China will utilize products imported from other countries to develop its own technology and strengthen its economic and military capabilities.

⑤ The U.S. Congress and other parties have said that U.S. chip design software is being used for China's weapons development. Some observers believe that exports of semiconductor manufacturing equipment from Japan and the Netherlands have boosted China's production capacity.

⑥ A multilateral system known as the Wassenaar Arrangement controls the export of conventional weapons, and related goods and technology. More than 40 countries, including Japan, the United States and Russia, have joined the arrangement, but with their own separate interests, it takes time to decide on the objects to be controlled.

U.S. Congress　米国議会

chip design software
半導体設計ソフト

Wassenaar Arrangement
ワッセナー協約（平和を乱
す恐れのある国に対する通
常兵器や関連技術の輸出規
制を目的とした国際輸出管
理機構）

⑦ To swiftly facilitate regulations, Japan and the United States hope to establish a new framework for a small number of countries with advanced technology.

⑧ The U.S. government has strictly restricted exports to many Chinese companies, including telecoms equipment giant Huawei Technologies Co. However, Washington has concluded there is a limit to what it can do on its own and a multilateral framework is necessary.

⑨ The Japanese government also believes that a new framework among countries with similar level of technology would be effective. Japan's active involvement in discussions on export controls is expected to help the country more readily predict the impact on Japanese companies.

⑩ In 1949, Western nations established the Coordinating Committee for Multilateral Export Controls (CoCom) — which was dissolved in 1994 — to prevent the outflow of technology that would strengthen the military power of communist countries, such as the then Soviet Union.

⑪ The new framework could develop into a modern version of CoCom, against the rise of China.

telecoms equipment giant 通信機器大手
Huawei Technologies Co. 華為技術（ファーウェイ）
Washington 米国政府（米国の首都があるところから）

then Soviet Union 当時のソビエト連邦

📰 column　その他の新聞英語の特徴

新聞英語に見られるその他の特徴として、次の２つを挙げることができます。

① 発言者・報告者の名前は発言・報告内容の後に置かれることが多い。
　　例１：South Africa's legal lion breeding ..., an animal welfare group warned ...
　　例２：Tigers are not native to South Africa and ..., the organization said.
② 補足説明の挿入が多い。
　　例１：the renowned Egyptologist Zahi Hawass, a former antiquities minister, the ...
　　例２：The mummy discovered in Luxor, Southern Egypt, is the only one not ...
これらの特徴は、限られたスペースの中で読み手が効率的に要点を把握できるよう配慮した結果生まれたと考えられます。

Task　Unit 5 の記事（NASA aims to make observations ...）を読み、①の特徴が見られる部分に＿＿＿、②の特徴が見られる部分に＿＿＿＿を引きましょう

While reading 1 次に関して、記事を読んで分かったことをメモしましょう。

CoCom について

....

While reading 2 記事の中で次の情報が述べられている段落の番号を書きましょう。

1. 米国のバイデン政権が表明した内容： [   ]

2. ワッセナー協約の加盟国： [   ]

3. 米国政府が輸出規制を行っている中国の通信機器大手企業： [   ]

4. 1994 年に解体された委員会： [   ]

While reading 3 空欄に適切な単語を入れ、記事の要約を完成させましょう。
最初の文字がヒントとして示してあります。

The U.S. government has strictly restricted exports to many Chinese
1)c_____. However, there is a limit to what it can do on its own. The U.S. and Japanese governments thus are considering the creation of a multilateral 2)f_____ to regulate the export of advanced technology to China. They are currently specifying the 3)f_____ to be subject to regulation, which would likely include semiconductor manufacturing equipment, quantum cryptography and 4)a_____ intelligence. The United States and Japan want to cooperate with like-minded countries in 5)E_____.

While reading 4 3で空欄に入れた単語が正しいか、音声で確認しましょう。

🔊 1-67

While reading 5 記事が示唆する内容と合致すれば T、しなければ F を記入しましょう。

1. If a multilateral framework to regulate the export of advanced technology is created, quantum cryptography would not likely be exported to China. [   ]

2. More than 50 countries will join a new multilateral framework to regulate the export of advanced technology.   [   ]

3. The administration of U.S. President Joe Biden has concluded that other countries with advanced technology need to control the export of their technology.   [   ]

4. CoCom lasted for more than 50 years.   [   ]

◢ After reading 1 語句を並べ替えて英文を完成させましょう。間違った場合、解答欄に正しい答えを書くこと。

1. 西側諸国は技術の流出を防ぐために CoCom を設立した。

Western nations (of / to / CoCom / prevent / established / the outflow) technology.

予 想 ：..

....

解 答 ： *Western nations*

....*technology.*

2. 中国は民間部門の先端技術を軍事力の増強に利用しようとしている。

China (to / to / boost / seeks / utilize / private-sector technology) its military capabilities.

予 想 ：..

....

解 答 ： *China*

....*its military capabilities.*

3. 米国は人権侵害につながる技術の規制を行う予定だ。

The United States will (to / that / could / regulate / technology / contribute) human rights abuses.

予 想 ：..

....

解 答 ： *The United States will*

....*human rights abuses.*

4. 彼らは規制が必要な分野を具体的に挙げようとしている。

They are (be / to / to / subject / specifying / the fields) regulation.

予 想 ：..

解 答 ： *They are*..*regulation.*

 **After reading 2**　次の説明はどの語についてのものか、文中から抜き出して必要に応じ正しい形に直しましょう。最初の文字がヒントとして示してあります。

1. the business of selling and sending goods to other countries

2. new machines, equipment, and ways of doing things that are based on modern knowledge about science and computers

3. a substance, such as silicon, that allows some electric currents to pass through it, and is used in electronic equipment

4. something that you use to fight with or attack someone with, such as a knife, bomb, gun

5. the effect or influence that an event, situation, etc., has on someone or something

6. to formally end a parliament, business arrangement, marriage, etc

1. e＿＿＿＿	2. t＿＿＿＿	3. s＿＿＿＿
4. w＿＿＿＿	5. i＿＿＿＿	6. d＿＿＿＿

After reading 3　次の課題について、自分の考えを述べましょう。

軍事衝突を防ぐために、他国の文化を理解することは重要だと思いますか。またその理由は何ですか。あなたの考えを書いてみましょう。

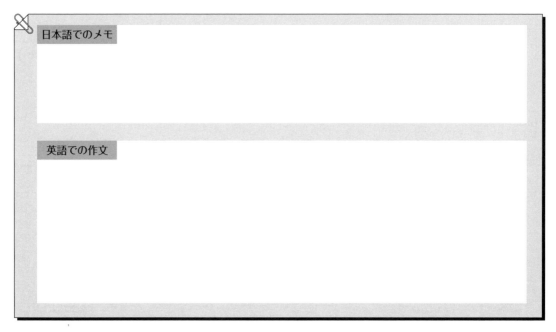

日本語でのメモ

英語での作文

UNIT 11

Greater support planned for tourism on remote islands

離島の観光業の支援強化が計画される

新型コロナウイルスの感染拡大の影響を受けた産業の一つが観光業です。特に、観光業を主要産業とする国境の離島では、宿泊客が激減し、島の経済にとって大打撃となっています。この Unit では、政府が離島の観光業の支援に乗り出すことを報じた記事を取り上げます。

🔲 *Before reading* 1

説明を読み、内容に関する理解を深めましょう。
また図からどんなことが言えるか考えましょう。

- 国土交通白書 2021 によれば、観光業 (tourism) は、旅行業、交通 (transportation) 産業、宿泊業、飲食産業、アミューズメント産業、土産品産業、旅行関連産業等の幅広い分野を含む産業であり、経済 (economy) に大きな影響を与える点で、我が国及び地域にとっての存続基盤と位置づけられています。

- 特定有人国境離島地域とは、領海及び排他的経済水域を管理する上で活動拠点となる有人の (inhabited) 離島 (remote island) のうち、「継続的な居住が可能となる環境の整備」が特に必要な島で構成される地域を指します。

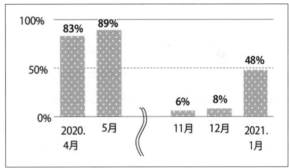

宿泊の 2020 年予約状況が 2019 年同月で
7 割以上現と回答した事業者の割合

出典：国土交通省ウェブサイト
(https://www.mlit.go.jp/hakusyo/mlit/r02/hakusho/r03/html/n1212000.html)

🔲 *Before reading* 2

日本語に対応する英語表現を選択肢から選び、○で囲みましょう。

1. 新型コロナウイルス　　　nobel coronavirus / novel coronavirus

2. 領海　　　untreated waters / territorial waters

3. 保全　　　perseverance / preservation

4. 特別措置法　　　special majors law / special measures law

5. 観光庁　　　Japan Travel Agency / Japan Tourism Agency

Greater support planned for tourism on remote islands

① The government has decided to strengthen its support for the promotion of tourism in areas designated as specific inhabited remote border islands, with a view to preserving territorial waters as well.

写真：田中正秋 / アフロ

② The economies of remote islands in particular have been hit hard by the decline in tourism due to the spread of the novel coronavirus. The initiative also aims to prevent the islands from losing residents and becoming uninhabitable, which will help preserve Japan's territorial waters.

③ The program will be launched as early as the end of March.

as early as ～
早くも～には

④ The government plans to subsidize 55% of a project cost to local governments for initiatives utilizing the unique tourism resources of remote islands, such as rich nature, history and fresh marine products.

⑤ For example, the government envisions tours that include a meal coupon for local seafood and a transportation ticket, and the development of new specialty foods.

⑥ The government also plans to support the training of tour guides and the creation of brochures.

⑦ Based on the special measures law for preserving inhabited remote island areas that came into force in 2016, the government has been promoting measures to maintain social and economic activities of remote border islands as part of efforts to prevent them from becoming uninhabited.

come into force
効力を生じる、発効する

⑧ The government is concerned that if the islands become uninhabited, it will become difficult to use them as a base of operations for security in the surrounding waters — which could hinder the preservation of territorial waters.

⑨ The government has designated 71 specific inhabited remote border islands in 29 municipalities of Tokyo and seven prefectures — including Rebun Island in Hokkaido, Sado Island in Niigata Prefecture and Tsushima Island in Nagasaki Prefecture — under the special measures law. The population of each island varies from about 50,000 to a few.

⑩ Tourism is a major earner on many islands, and its decline amid the coronavirus crisis has been deeper than the national average.

⑪ According to the Japan Tourism Agency, the number of travelers who stayed on remote islands declined about 75% in April-June 2021 from the same period in 2019. The number of travelers nationwide declined about 58% in the same period.

⑫ The sharp decline is believed to have been caused by limits on transportation to the islands and the reluctance of residents to accept visitors in fear of infection with the novel coronavirus.

⑬ The government is concerned that if tourism continues to be sluggish, more people will leave the islands, which could cause a further decline in the population.

Rebun Island
礼文島

Sado Island
佐渡島

Tsushima Island
対馬

in fear of ～
～を恐れて

🎧 While reading 1 次に関して、記事を読んで分かったことをメモしてみましょう。

1. 離島の観光業支援の内容

....

2. 離島の観光業衰退の原因

....

3. 観光業の衰退によって懸念されること

....

While reading 2 記事の中で次の情報が述べられている段落の番号を書きましょう。

1. 離島の観光業支援事業の開始予定時期：[   ]

2. 有人国境離島地域の保全に関する特別措置法が発効した年：[   ]

3. 観光業支援事業の対象となる有人国境離島の数：[   ]

4. 離島の観光客数減少を示す観光庁のデータ：[   ]

While reading 3 空欄に適切な単語または数字を入れ、記事の要約を完成させましょう。答えが単語の場合、最初の文字がヒントとして示してあります。

Tourism is a major earner on many islands, and its decline amid the coronavirus ¹⁾c_____ has been deeper than the national average. According to the Japan Tourism Agency, the number of travelers who stayed on remote islands declined about ²⁾____% in April-June 2021 from the same period in 2019. In order to prevent the islands from losing ³⁾r_____ and becoming uninhabitable, the government has decided to strengthen its support for the ⁴⁾p_____ of tourism in areas designated as specific inhabited remote border islands, with a view to preserving ⁵⁾t_____ waters as well.

While reading 4 3で空欄に入れた単語または数字が正しいか、音声で確認しましょう。

🔊 **2-08**

While reading 5 記事が示唆する内容と合致すれば T、しなければ F を記入しましょう。

1. The government will launch its support program before the start of fiscal 2022 at the earliest. [   ]

2. The government plans to cover more than half of a project cost to local governments for initiatives utilizing the unique tourism resources of remote islands. [   ]

3. The 29 municipalities of Tokyo have more than 70 specific inhabited remote border islands. [   ]

4. The number of travelers who stayed on remote islands declined 1.5 times more than the national average in April-June 2021. [   ]

 **After reading 1** 語句を並べ替えて英文を完成させましょう。間違った場合、解答欄に正しい答えを書くこと。

1. 有人国境離島地域の保全に関する特別措置法は 2016 年に発効した。

The special measures law for (in / came / into / force / preserving / inhabited remote island areas) 2016.

予想： ....

解答： *The special measures law for* ....

....*2016.*...................................

2. 離島の経済は観光業の衰退により大きな打撃を受けた。

The economies of remote islands (by / hit / been / hard / have / the decline) in tourism.

予想： ....

解答： *The economies of remote islands* ....

....*in tourism.*..

3. 急激な衰退は離島への移動制限によって引き起こされたと考えられている。

The sharp decline (is / to / have / been / caused / believed) by limits on transportation to remote islands.

予想： ....

解答： *The sharp decline* ....

.................*by limits on transportation to remote islands.*...............

4. その計画にはその島々の住民の減少を防ぐねらいがある。

The plan (to / aims / from / losing / prevent / the islands) residents.

予想： ....

解答： *The plan* ....

residents....

 **After reading 2** 次の説明はどの語についてのものか、文中から抜き出して必要に応じ正しい形に直しましょう。最初の文字がヒントとして示してあります。

1. the business of providing things for people to do, places for them to stay, etc., while they are on holiday

2. the official line that separates two countries, states, or areas, or the area close to this line

3. to imagine something that you think might happen in the future, especially something that you think will be good

4. a thin book giving information or advertising something

5. to make it difficult for something to develop or succeed

6. moving or reacting more slowly than normal

1. t _____	2. b _____	3. e _____
4. b _____	5. h _____	6. s _____

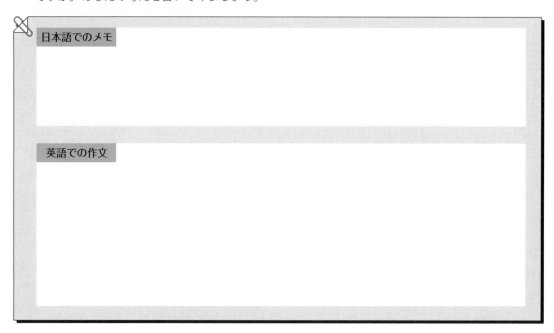 **After reading 3** 次の課題について、自分の考えを述べましょう。

離島に観光客を呼び寄せるためにどのような対策が必要だと思いますか。またそう思う理由は何ですか。あなたの考えを書いてみましょう。

日本語でのメモ

英語での作文

UNIT 12

Govt eyes new guidelines for huge quake in Tokyo area

政府、首都での巨大地震に備えた新ガイドラインを検討

 いつ発生してもおかしくないと言われている「首都直下地震」。みなさんは、この地震が起きた時にどんな行動をとるか決めていますか。この Unit では、政府が首都直下地震に備えた新たなガイドラインの検討に乗り出したことを報じた記事を取り上げます。

⊞ Before reading 1 説明を読み、内容に関する理解を深めましょう。
また図からどんなことが言えるか考えましょう。

- 首都直下地震に関しては、2015 年に「首都直下地震緊急対策推進基本計画」が作成され（devised）ています。
- この指針（guidelines）では、大地震（major earthquake）発生後の 3 日間は職場（workplace）や学校で待機するよう呼びかけています。また、「道路交通渋滞（congestion）、生活物資の不足を見越した上で、各家庭や企業等における『最低 3 日間、推奨 1 週間』分の水・食料等の備蓄に努める」との文言もあります。

主要活断層帯の概略位置図

出典：内閣府ホームページ
(https://www.bousai.go.jp/kyoiku/
hokenkyousai/jishin.html)

⊞ Before reading 2 日本語に対応する英語表現を選択肢から選び、○で囲みましょう。

1. 公共交通機関　　　　　public transparence ／ public transportation

2. 二次災害　　　　　　　secondary disaster ／ alternative disaster

3. 将棋倒し　　　　　　　stamper ／ stampede

4. 内閣府　　　　　　　　the Cabined Office ／ the Cabinet Office

5. 東日本大震災　　　　　the Great East Japan Earthquake ／
　　　　　　　　　　　　the Great Eastern Japan Earthquake

Govt eyes new guidelines for huge quake in Tokyo area

写真：読売新聞社

① The government plans to review a policy regarding what people should do in the event of a major earthquake in the greater Tokyo area, The Yomiuri Shimbun has learned.

the greater Tokyo area
首都圏

② According to sources, a three-stage plan is being considered to determine the course of action people should take if they are not at home when disaster strikes, regarding how, when and whether to return home. The current policy calls for people to remain in situ for three days if a disaster occurs when they are at such locations as their workplace or school.

in situ
もとの場所に、そのままの場所に

③ The government plans to devise as early as this summer more flexible measures that will utilize big data and other tools and incorporate them into its guidelines.

④ According to an estimate by the Cabinet Office, in the event of an earthquake measuring 7 on the Japanese seismic intensity scale — the highest level — about 6.95 million people in Tokyo and its four neighboring prefectures would be unable to return home, about 4.15 million of whom would be stranded in the capital.

seismic intensity scale
震度階

⑤ After the Great East Japan Earthquake on March 11, 2011, about 5.15 million people in the Tokyo metropolitan area were unable to return home.

⑥ Under the current policy, people would be urged not to return home for 72 hours after a major disaster to prioritize rescue efforts during a period regarded as a critical window,

critical window
決定的に重要な期間

68

after which the survival rate falls sharply.

⑦ There would be mass congestion if people tried to return home on foot, by taxi or other means, which would likely interfere with emergency activities and possibly trigger
35 secondary disasters such as stampedes.

⑧ Guidelines devised in 2015 called for administrative bodies to "focus their efforts on helping people return home on the fourth day of a disaster or later."

administrative body
行政機関

⑨ The Tokyo metropolitan government has also
40 encouraged people to "remain at their workplaces, schools or other safe places for three days without moving around unnecessarily."

The Tokyo metropolitan government
東京都

⑩ Improvements to earthquake resistance of station buildings and railway lines in recent years have meant that
45 public transportation systems have been able to resume operations within three days following a disaster in some cases.

⑪ As disaster damage varies from region to region, the government has concluded that it is not realistic to
50 uniformly request people to remain in situ, according to a Cabinet Office official.

⑫ In light of this, the guidelines will be revised to allow people to return home depending on the disaster situation, to the extent that it does not interfere with emergency
55 activities, according to the sources.

🖎 **While reading 1**　　次に関して、記事を読んで分かったことをメモしてみましょう。

1.　首都直下地震が発生した場合の帰宅困難者の推計

....

2.　東日本大震災が発生した際に帰宅できなかった人の数

....

3.　現行の指針が出されてからの状況の変化

....

While reading 2 記事の中で次の情報が述べられている段落の番号を書きましょう。

1. 政府がガイドラインの見直しを計画している時期：[   ]

2. 現行のガイドラインが作成された年：[   ]

3. 東京都が勧めている地震発生後の行動：[   ]

4. 内閣府の職員の発言：[   ]

While reading 3 空欄に適切な単語または数字を入れ、記事の要約を完成させましょう。答えが単語の場合、最初の文字がヒントとして示してあります。

The government plans to review a policy regarding what people should do in the event of a major earthquake in the 1)g_____ Tokyo area. Under the current policy, people would be urged not to return home for 2)_____ hours after a major disaster. However, improvements to earthquake 3)r_____ of station buildings and railway lines in recent years have meant that public transportation systems have been able to resume 4)o_____ within three days following a disaster in some cases. In light of this, the guidelines will be revised to allow people to return home depending on the disaster 5)s_____.

While reading 4 3で空欄に入れた単語または数字が正しいか、音声で確認しましょう。

🔊 2-15

While reading 5 記事が示唆する内容と合致すれば T、しなければ F を記入しましょう。

1. In the event of a major earthquake, more people in the greater Tokyo area would be unable to return home than when the Great East Japan Earthquake happened.   [   ]

2. In order to save the lives of people in need of rescue, the first three days after a major disaster is a crucial period.   [   ]

3. More than ten years have passed since the current guidelines were devised.   [   ]

4. The Japanese government and the Tokyo metropolitan government have the same policy on how many days people should remain in situ.   [   ]

70

 **After reading 1** 　語句を並べ替えて英文を完成させましょう。間違った場合、解答欄に正しい答えを書くこと。

1. ガイドラインは行政機関に対して人々の帰宅支援の取組に集中するよう求めていた。

   The guidelines (to / for / focus / called / their efforts / administrative bodies) on helping people return home.

   予 想 : ....

   解 答 : *The guidelines* ....
   .... *on helping people return home.*

2. 人々にその場にいるよう求めるのは現実的ではない。

   It (is / to / not / people / request / realistic) to remain in situ.

   予 想 : ....

   解 答 : *It* .... *to remain in situ.*

3. 大規模渋滞は（人々の）将棋倒しといった二次災害のきっかけになるかもしれない。

   Mass congestion (as / such / would / trigger / stampedes / secondary disasters).

   予 想 : ....
   ....

   解 答 : *Mass congestion* ....
   ....

4. 我々は臨界期と考えられている時期に救助の取り組みを優先する必要がある。

   We need to (as / during / regarded / prioritize / a period / rescue efforts) a critical window.

   予 想 : ....
   ....

   解 答 : *We need to* ....
   .... *a critical window.*

 **After reading 2**　次の説明はどの語についてのものか、文中から抜き出して必要に応じ正しい形に直しましょう。最初の文字がヒントとして示してあります。

1. a way of doing something that has been officially agreed and chosen by a political party, a business, or another organization

2. a calculation of the value, size, amount, etc., of something made using the information that you have, which may not be complete

3. to leave somebody in a place from which they have no way of leaving

4. to put several things, problems, etc., in order of importance, so that you can deal with the most important ones first

5. the problem of too much traffic in a place

6. a situation in which a group of people or large animals such as horses suddenly start running in the same direction, especially because they are frightened or excited

1. p _____	2. e _____	3. s _____
4. p _____	5. c _____	6. s _____

 **After reading 3**　次の課題について、自分の考えを述べましょう。

大きな地震が起きた際、最初の1時間にどのような行動をとりたいと思っていますか。またそう思う理由は何ですか。あなたの考えを書いてみましょう。

日本語でのメモ

英語での作文

Disabled artists increasingly getting noticed by consumers

障害者アーティスト、徐々に消費者に認知される

みなさんは障害を持つアーティストが作った芸術作品を目にしたり、購入したことはありますか。この Unit では、障害のあるアーティストの社会参加を支援したり、芸術作品を商品化する動きが広がっていることを報じた記事を取り上げます。

🔲 Before reading 1

説明を読み、内容に関する理解を深めましょう。
また図からどんなことが言えるか考えましょう。

- 近年、発達障害（developmental disability）や精神障害（mental disorder）を持つ人々の社会参画（participation in society）を促す動きが広がっています。
- 障害者アーティスト（disabled artist）による作品の販売を通じて、彼らが消費者（consumer）とつながる（connect）だけでなく、自立する（independent）ことが可能になります。

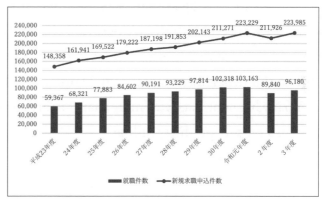

障害者の求職と就職の状況

出典：厚生労働省「令和3年度障害者職業紹介状況等」より作成

🔲 Before reading 2

日本語に対応する英語表現を選択肢から選び、○で囲みましょう。

1. 自閉症　　　　　autism / autoimmune
2. 福祉施設　　　　welfare facility / outpatient facility
3. 非営利団体　　　nonprofit organization / unofficial organization
4. 芸術性　　　　　artistry / artificiality
5. 個展　　　　　　solo exhibition / private exhibition

Disabled artists increasingly getting noticed by consumers

① OSAKA — Efforts to support artistic endeavors by people with disabilities are gaining steam.

② In addition to encouraging their participation in society, more products that demonstrate disabled people's artistry and sense of design are hitting the market, with last year's Tokyo Paralympic Games giving these initiatives even more momentum.

gain steam
活発化する

artistry
芸術性

hit the market
市場に出る

'Cute and cool'

③ Displays of colorful handkerchiefs, ties and umbrellas at a Heralbony Co. pop-up shop in Kyoto include profiles of the artists who designed them and other information.

④ Morioka-based Heralbony sells products made with art created by people with disabilities, and the firm opened its first pop-up shop in Kansai in December for a two-month run at the department store Fujii Daimaru in Kyoto. The company has contracts with more than 150 artists nationwide and also sells its products online.

pop-up shop
ポップアップ・ショップ［ストア］（空き店舗などに突如出店し、一定期間で突然消えてしまう店舗）

Fujii Daimaru
藤井大丸（百貨店）

⑤ "The splendor of the art is our foundation. This isn't a charity. We have items people think are cute and cool," said a company spokesperson.

⑥ A 32-year-old Kyoto native with autism, provides Heralbony with designs for handkerchiefs and stoles. He was discovered at a local gallery when he was 18 years old and is now a popular artist who holds solo exhibitions in Japan and abroad.

⑦ His mother said: "Drawing makes him happy. It's rewarding and leads him to new challenges."

Corporate partnerships

⑧ Traditionally, creative endeavors by people with disabilities have been part of rehabilitation services provided by welfare facilities, but in the 2000s social welfare organizations started opening museums in places like Shiga and Hiroshima prefectures dedicated to their art.

⑨ These efforts have been propelled by "art brut" that features works by outsiders to the art world, including people with disabilities. In recent years, designs have been turned into products through partnerships with companies, which has helped connect artists with consumers.

⑩ Last year, the nonprofit organization Inclusive Japan, which operates a job assistance office in Ehime Prefecture, used crowdfunding to launch an initiative to produce reusable shopping bags with Tokyo-based Toppan Inc.

Toppan Inc.
凸版印刷株式会社

⑪ The office has about 50 people with developmental disabilities and mental disorders who help create the bags, which were displayed at a members-only cafe.

⑫ "I hope this will provide an opportunity for them to open their hearts to society," a person handling the initiative said.

⑬ The Able Art Company in Nara, which is run jointly by three NPOs, matches manufacturers with artists it recruits to work on projects including sake labels and T-shirts. The goal is to get artists paid and help them become more independent.

Able Art Company
エイブルアート・カンパニー

 **While reading 1**　次に関して、記事を読んで分かったことをメモしてみましょう。

ヘラルボニーについて

1. ヘラルボニーの本社がある場所：[　　　]

2. 自閉症を持つ京都出身のアーティストの年齢：[　　　]

3. 2000 年代に社会福祉団体が障害者アートに特化した博物館を開設した県：[　　　]

4. 3 つの NPO が共同運営する奈良市の会社の名前：[　　　]

Traditionally, $^{1)}$c＿＿＿＿＿ endeavors by people with disabilities have been part of rehabilitation services provided by welfare facilities. However, in the $^{2)}$＿＿＿＿s social welfare organizations started opening museums in places like Shiga and Hiroshima prefectures dedicated to their art. These efforts have been propelled by "art brut" that features works by $^{3)}$o＿＿＿＿＿ to the art world, including people with disabilities. In recent years, designs have been turned into $^{4)}$p＿＿＿＿＿ through partnerships with companies, which has helped connect artists with $^{5)}$c＿＿＿＿＿ .

🔊 2-22

1. The pop-up shop which Heralbony opened will have been closed by March, 2022.　[　　　]

2. The artists with whom Heralbony has contracts are all from Morioka.　[　　　]

3. The works which the 32-year-old Kyoto native with autism created have been exhibited in a foreign country.　[　　　]

4. Some museums in Shiga and Hiroshima prefectures have been exhibiting works created by disabled artists only for more than 10 years.　[　　　]

1. その会社は障害を持つ人々によるアートで作られた商品を販売している。

The company sells products made with (by / art / with / people / created / disabilities).

予想： ....

解答： *The company sells products made with*

....

2. 私たちには人々がカッコイイと思うアイテムがある。

We (are / cool / have / items / think / people).

予想： ....

解答： *We*

3. この取り組みは障害のあるアーティストたちが社会に心を開く機会を提供するだろう。

This initiative will (to / for / open / provide / an opportunity / disabled artists) their hearts to society.

予想： ....

解答： *This initiative will*

their hearts to society.

4. 目標はアーティストたちがより独立できるよう支援することだ。

The goal (is / to / help / more / become / artists) independent.

予想： ....

解答： *The goal*

 次の説明はどの語についてのものか、文中から抜き出して必要に応じ正しい形に直しましょう。最初の文字がヒントとして示してあります。

1. an object with a round folding frame of long straight pieces of metal covered with material, that you use to protect yourself from the rain or from hot sun.

2. a short description that gives important details about a person, a group of people, or a place

3. a mental disorder that makes people unable to communicate properly, or to form relationships

4. a long straight piece of cloth or fur that a woman wears across her shoulders

5. a large building where people can see famous pieces of art

6. a small restaurant where you can buy drinks and simple meals

1. u _____	2. p _____	3. a _____
4. s _____	5. g _____	6. c _____

After reading 3 次の課題について、自分の考えを述べましょう。

障害を持つ方の社会参加を支援するため、どんなことが必要だと思いますか。またそう思う理由は何ですか。あなたの考えを書いてみましょう。

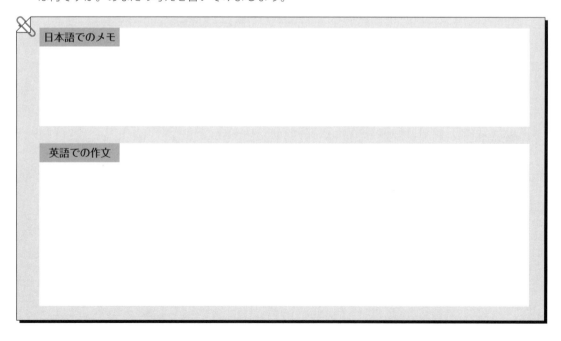

日本語でのメモ

英語での作文

Time capsule from Confederate statue reveals US Civil War artifacts

UNIT 14

南軍の像からタイムカプセル、南北戦争の遺物を見せる

みなさんは世界史の授業等で米国の南北戦争について学びましたか。この Unit では、南北戦争における南軍司令官であったロバート・E・リー将軍像の台座の下からタイプカプセルが発見されたことを報じた記事を取り上げます。

Before reading 1

説明を読み、内容に関する理解を深めましょう。
また図からどんなことが言えるか考えましょう。

- 今回発見された銅（copper）製のタイムカプセル（time capsule）は、南軍を率いた将軍（general）の像（statue）の台座（pedestal）に埋まった（embedded）状態で発見されました。

- タイムカプセルの中には、米国の南北戦争（Civil War）当時の銃弾（bullet）や紙幣（banknote）などが入っていました。

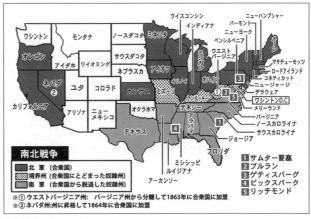

南北戦争の北軍と南軍

Before reading 2

日本語に対応する英語表現を選択肢から選び、◯で囲みましょう。

1. 通貨　　　　　　　curacy / currency

2. 棺　　　　　　　　casket / cascade

3. 兵器、軍需品　　　ordnance / ordinance

4. 奴隷制賛成　　　　pro-slavery / anti-slavery

5. 南部連合国の　　　Federal / Confederate

Time capsule from Confederate statue reveals US Civil War artifacts

写真提供：ロイター / アフロ

① A time capsule buried 130 years ago in the base of a statue of a Confederate general revealed its secrets on Tuesday—bullets, buttons and currency from the 1861-65 US Civil War along with other artifacts.

② The copper box was found Monday embedded in the stone pedestal of a statue of General Robert E. Lee, who commanded the Army of Northern Virginia during the bloody conflict between the North and the South.

③ Lee's bronze statue was erected in 1890 in Richmond, the Virginia city that was the capital of the pro-slavery South during the Civil War. It was taken down in September, one of a number of Confederate monuments removed in recent months.

④ The time capsule was opened on Tuesday by conservators at the Department of Historic Resources in Richmond and the contents were in relatively good condition, having suffered only a bit of water damage.

⑤ "It's in better shape than we had expected," said Kate Ridgway, the state archaeological conservator, at a ceremony during which the 14×14×8 inch (35×35×20 centimeter) box was opened before live television cameras.

⑥ "We thought everything would be soup and it's not soup so that's great," Ridgway said.

⑦ An 1887 article in a Richmond newspaper had listed some of the items secreted away in the time capsule and they matched some of those found on Tuesday.

Robert E. Lee
ロバート・エドワード・リー（米国の軍人。南北戦争時の南軍の総指揮官）

Army of Northern Virginia
北バージニア軍（南北戦争東部戦線において南軍の主力として戦った軍）

Department of Historic Resources
歴史資源局（州政府事務所）

soup
混沌とした状況

secreted away
秘密にされて

⑧ The newspaper article had mentioned what would have been a rare 1865 photograph of assassinated president Abraham Lincoln in his casket but no such photo was found.

35 ⑨ What was found was an engraving from the April 29, 1865 edition of Harper's Weekly depicting a woman weeping next to Lincoln's casket.

Bullets, banknotes, buttons, coins

40 ⑩ Several Civil War bullets known as Minie balls were also found in the container along with a piece of wood with a bullet lodged in it.

⑪ There was a shell fragment said to be from the 1862 Battle of Fredericksburg.

45 ⑫ "We were actually afraid this was live ordnance," Ridgway said. "This was part of the reason we had the bomb squad come out. It is, in fact, not live."

⑬ A small Confederate flag and a Masonic symbol carved out of wood were also found enclosed in an envelope.

50 ⑭ The wood used for the carvings reportedly came from a tree that grew over the grave of another famed Confederate general, Thomas Stonewall Jackson.

⑮ Also found in the box were Confederate banknotes, buttons with the seal of the state of Virginia and a bundle
55 of 12 copper coins.

Abraham Lincoln
エイブラハム・リンカーン
(アメリカ合衆国第16代大
統領，1809-1865)
engraving
製版
Harper's Weekly
ハーパーズ・ウィークリー
(1857-1916年に発行され
た米国の政治雑誌)

Minie ball
ミニエ式銃弾

lodged
撃ち込まれた

shell fragment
榴弾の破片

Battle of Fredericksburg
フレデリックスバーグの戦い

bomb squad
爆発物処理班

Masonic
フリーメーソンの

Thomas Stonewall
Jackson
トーマス・ストーンウォー
ル・ジャクソン

⊚ While reading 1 次に関して、記事を読んで分かったことをメモしてみましょう。

1. タイムカプセルが発見された場所や時間、発見時の状況

....

2. タイムカプセルの中身

....

While reading 2 事の中で次の情報が述べられている段落の番号を書きましょう。

1. リー将軍の像が建てられた年：[　　　]
2. タイムカプセルのサイズ：[　　　]
3. 発見された『ハーパーズ・ウィークリー』の製版にあった日付：[　　　]
4. フレデリックスバーグの戦いが起きた年：[　　　]

While reading 3 空欄に適切な単語または数字を入れ、記事の要約を完成させましょう。
答えが単語の場合、最初の文字がヒントとして示してあります。

A statue of ¹⁾G_____ Robert E. Lee, who commanded the Army of Northern Virginia during the bloody conflict between the North and the ²⁾S_____, was erected in 1890 in Richmond, and the statue was taken down in September, 2021. On December 27, 2021, a time capsule buried ³⁾_____ years ago was found embedded in the stone pedestal of the statue. The time capsule was opened the next day by ⁴⁾c_____ at the Department of Historic Resources in Richmond. The conservators found bullets, buttons and currency from the 1861-65 US ⁵⁾C_____War along with other artifacts.

While reading 4 CDを聞き、3で空欄に入れた単語または数字が正しいか確認しましょう。

 2-29

While reading 5 記事が示唆する内容と合致すれば T、しなければ F を記入しましょう。

1. The statue of General Robert E. Lee was erected more than 30 years after the Civil War.　[　　　]

2. The statue of General Robert E. Lee was taken down in September, 2022.　[　　　]

3. An article in a Richmond paper which referred to the time capsule was published five years after Lincoln was assassinated.　[　　　]

4. Ridgway and her colleagues thought what was found in the time capsule might explode.　[　　　]

 語句を並べ替えて英文を完成させましょう。間違った場合、解答欄に
正しい答えを書くこと。

1. 銅製の箱はある像の台座の中に埋まった状態で発見された。

The copper box (in / of / was / found / embedded / the stone pedestal) a
statue.

予 想 : ....

解 答 : *The copper box* ....

a statue.

2. タイムカプセルは私たちが予想していたよりもよい状態だった。

The time capsule (in / we / had / was / than / better shape) expected.

予 想 : ....

解 答 : *The time capsule* ....

expected.

3. ハーパーズ・ウィークリーの製版はリンカーンの棺の横で泣く女性を描いていた。

Harper's Weekly (to / next / weeping / depicted / a woman / Lincoln's casket).

予 想 : ....

解 答 : *Harper's Weekly* ....

....

4. 彫刻に用いられた木材はそのお墓の上で育った木を用いていた。

The wood (for / came / from / used / a tree / the carvings) that grew over the
grave.

予 想 : ....

解 答 : *The wood*

that grew over the grave.

 **After reading 2** 次の説明はどの語についてのものか、文中から抜き出して必要に応じ正しい形に直しましょう。最初の文字がヒントとして示してあります。

1. an image of a person or animal that is made in solid material such as stone or metal and is usually large

2. an officer of very high rank in the army or air force

3. an object such as a tool, weapon, etc., that was made in the past and is historically important

4. a person who is responsible for repairing and preserving works of art, buildings and other things of cultural interest

5. a piece of writing about a particular subject in a newspaper or magazine

6. the police department responsible for dealing with a particular kind of crime

| 1. s _____ | 2. g _____ | 3. a _____ |
| 4. c _____ | 5. a _____ | 6. s _____ |

After reading 3 次の課題について、自分の考えを述べましょう。

もしみなさんが100年後の人々にタイムカプセルを残すとしたら、カプセルにどんなものを入れますか。またそれを選んだ理由は何ですか。あなたの考えを書いてみましょう。

日本語でのメモ

英語での作文

Mother remembers 'brutal' soldiers who terrorised Bucha

母親、ブチャを恐怖に陥れた「残忍な」兵士を記憶

 ロシアによるウクライナ侵攻は世界に大きな影響を与えていますが、その中でもブチャでの虐殺に関する報道は衝撃的でした。この Unit では、地元住民が虐殺に関して話した内容を取り上げた記事を紹介します。

Before reading 1

説明を読み、内容に関する理解を深めましょう。また図からどんなことが言えるか考えましょう

- ロシア軍（Russian forces）はウクライナへの侵攻（invasion）後数日でブチャ（Bucha）を占領（occupation）し、占領は1ヵ月続きました。

- ブチャでは民間人の衣類（civilian clothing）を身に付けた多数の遺体が発見されています。

- ロシアは民間人の殺害（civilian killings）に関する告発（accusation）を否定しています。

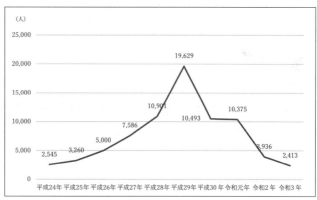

難民認定申請者数の推移（国内）

(人)

25,000 — 20,000 — 15,000 — 10,000 — 5,000 — 0

19,629
10,901 10,493 10,375
7,586
5,000   3,936
3,260   2,413
2,545

平成24年 平成25年 平成26年 平成27年 平成28年 平成29年 平成30年 令和元年 令和2年 令和3年

「令和3年における難民認定者数等について」（出入国在留管理庁ホームページ）をもとに作成
(https://www.moj.go.jp/isa/content/001372236.pdf)

Before reading 2

日本語に対応する英語表現を選択肢から選び、○で囲みましょう。

1. 地下室　　　　　　　cellar / collar

2. 虐殺　　　　　　　　massacre / masscult

3. 砲撃　　　　　　　　bombardment / bomb arming

4. 国家保安機関　　　　national service / security service

5. （兵士の）作業服　　fatigues / sailor suit

Mother remembers 'brutal' soldiers who terrorised Bucha

① A couple of weeks into the Russian occupation of Bucha, local resident Olena sensed a turn for the worse when older, rougher soldiers appeared and began to spread fear in the town.

② "They were brutal compared to the younger soldiers who captured the town at the start of the invasion," said the 43-year-old mother of two.

③ "Right in front of my eyes, they fired on a man who was going to get food at the supermarket," said Olena, who did not wish to give her second name.

④ Located 30 kilometres (19 miles) northwest of Kyiv's city centre, the town of Bucha was occupied by Russian forces on February 27 in the opening days of the war and remained under their control for a month.

⑤ After the bombardments stopped, Ukrainian forces were able to retake the town on Thursday.

⑥ Large numbers of bodies of men in civilian clothing have since been found in the streets.

⑦ Throughout March, Olena lived with her children, 7 and 9 years old, in a cellar with no electricity under a four-storey housing block, along with other residents.

⑧ "There was no Ukrainian army in town, only the territorial defense made up mostly of unarmed guards from local businesses. And then they fled when the Russians arrived," she said.

⑨ "At the beginning, there were mostly young (Russian)

写真：ロイター / アフロ

Bucha
ブチャ（ウクライナの首都キーウの北西に位置する都市）

fire on ～
～に発砲する

Kyiv
キーウ（ウクライナの首都）

four-storey housing block
4階建ての団地

territorial defense
領土防衛（隊）

soldiers. Then, two weeks later, there were others, older ones. They were more than 40 years old."

⑩ "They were brutal. They mistreated everyone. And that's when the massacres started," she said, before pausing, a dark, thoughtful look on her face.

35

⑪ On Monday, Russia categorically rejected all accusations in relation to civilian killings.

in relation to ～
～に関連して

'Lying in blood'

40

⑫ According to Olena, the older soldiers were very well equipped and wore black and dark green uniforms as opposed to standard Russian army fatigues.

as opposed to ～
～に反対して

⑬ "There were some good guys among the Russian soldiers and there were some very rough men, especially officers from the FSB, the Russian security services," said Olena, who was dressed in a red beanie, a fleece jacket, tracksuit bottoms and trainers.

45

FSB
連邦保安局

beanie
ビーニー帽（頭にぴったり
した丸い小型の帽子）

⑭ "I was going up to the soldiers to ask them what I should feed my children with and they brought us rations and food."

50

⑮ "It was they who told us that it was the FSB that had banned us from moving around, that they were very violent special forces. It was Russians saying this about the Russians!" she said.

⑯ Only women were allowed to leave to fetch water or food. The men were not permitted to go out into the streets and had to stay where they were.

55

 **While reading 1** 　次に関して、記事を読んで分かったことをメモしてみましょう。

ブチャについて

記事の中で次の情報が述べられている段落の番号を書きましょう。

1. オレナさんの年齢：［　　　］

2. キーウ中心部からブチャまでの距離：［　　　］

3. オレナさんの子ども達の年齢：［　　　］

4. オレナさんの服装：［　　　］

While reading 3 空欄に適切な単語または数字を入れ、記事の要約を完成させましょう。答えが単語の場合、最初の文字がヒントとして示してあります。

Located 30 kilometres northwest of Kyiv's city centre, the town of Bucha was occupied by Russian forces on February **1)**_____ in the opening days of the war and remained under their control for a **2)**m_____. According to a local resident, two weeks after the occupation, older, rougher **3)**s_____ appeared and began to spread fear in the town. They were brutal and mistreated people. After the **4)**b_____ stopped, Ukrainian forces were able to retake the town on March 31, 2022. Large numbers of bodies of men in civilian clothing have since been found in the **5)**s_____.

While reading 4 3で空欄に入れた単語または数字が正しいか、音声で確認しましょう。

🔊 2-38

While reading 5 記事が示唆する内容と合致すれば T、しなければ F を記入しましょう。

1. Olena had two children in her late twenties.　［　　　］

2. There was a big battle between the territorial defense and Russian forces.　［　　　］

3. According to Olena, there were no massacres in Bucha in early March.　［　　　］

4. Standard Russian soldiers wore black and dark green uniforms.　［　　　］

語句を並べ替えて英文を完成させましょう。間違った場合、解答欄に正しい答えを書くこと。

1. 2人の子どもを持つ43歳の母親は自身の名前を伝えるのを望まなかった。

   The 43-year-old mother of two children (to / did / not / wish / give / her name).

   予 想 : ....

   解 答 : *The 43-year-old mother of two children*

   ....

2. その母親は4階建ての団地の下にある電気のない地下室で生活した。

   The mother (in / with / lived / under / a cellar / no electricity) a four-story housing block.

   予 想 : ....

   解 答 : *The mother*

   a four-story housing block.

3. 若い兵士達は我々に移動を禁止したのはFSBだと教えてくれた。

   Young soldiers told us that (it / had / was / that / banned / the FSB) us from moving around.

   予 想 : ....

   解 答 : *Young soldiers told us that*

   us from moving around.

4. ロシアは市民の殺害に関する全ての告発を否定した。

   Russia (in / to / rejected / relation / all accusations / civilian killings).

   予 想 : ....

   解 答 : *Russia*

   ....

 **After reading 2** 次の説明はどの語についてのものか、文中から抜き出して必要に応じ正しい形に直しましょう。最初の文字がヒントとして示してあります。

1. the act of moving into a country, town, etc., and taking control of it using military force; the period of time during which a country, town, etc., is controlled in this way

2. a member of the army of a country, especially someone who is not an officer

3. a very large shop that sells food, drinks, and things that people need regularly in their homes

4. a room under a house or other buildings, often used for storing things

5. the killing of a large number of people especially in a cruel way

6. a statement saying that someone is guilty of a crime or of doing something wrong

1. o _____	2. s _____	3. s _____
4. c _____	5. m _____	6. a _____

After reading 3 次の課題について、自分の考えを述べましょう。

もしみなさんが兵士として占領地域に派遣された場合、どういう行動をとりますか。またその行動を選択する理由は何ですか。あなたの考えを書いてみましょう。

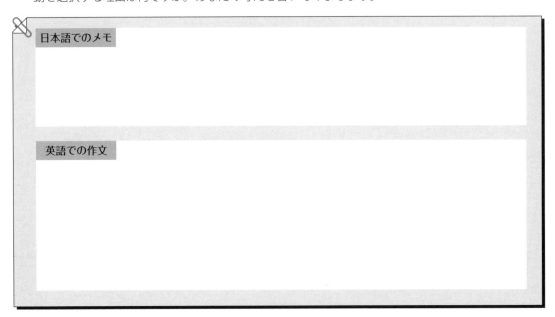

日本語でのメモ

英語での作文

UNIT 16

Fake social media accounts aimed at Ukraine, says Meta

メタ、ウクライナを標的とした偽 SNS アカウントを報告

ロシアによるウクライナへの攻撃は、軍事だけでなく情報操作においても行われています。この Unit では、ロシアがどのような手段でウクライナを標的とした偽情報キャンペーンを展開していたのかを報じた記事を紹介します。

Before reading 1　説明を読み、内容に関する理解を深めましょう。また図からどんなことが言えるか考えましょう。

- クリミア半島（Crimea）にある複数の報道機関（media organization）が、ロシア情報機関（intelligence service）からの指示で偽情報（disinformation）を発信したとされています。

- これらの報道機関は 2020 年の米大統領選（US presidential election）へ関与しようとしたことで制裁を課されて（sanctioned）います。

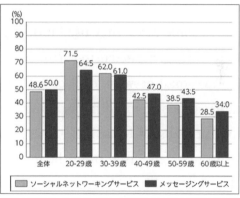

日本国内の SNS 及びメッセージサービスの利用状況

出典：総務省（2021）「ウィズコロナにおけるデジタル活用の実態と利用者意識の変化に関する調査研究」
(https://www.soumu.go.jp/johotsusintokei/whitepaper/ja/r03/html/nd111110.html)

Before reading 2　日本語に対応する英語表現を選択肢から選び、○で囲みましょう。

1. （簡単な）発表、報告　　　briefing / bristling

2. フィッシングメール　　　fishing email / phishing email

3. 軍関係者　　　miliary figure / military figure

4. 開始命令　　　marching order / overarching order

5. 独立系報道機関　　　independent news entity / indispensable news entity

91

Fake social media accounts aimed at Ukraine, says Meta

① Pro-Russia groups are orchestrating misinformation campaigns on social media, using fake profiles or hacked accounts to paint Ukraine as a feeble pawn of Western duplicity, Meta said Sunday.

5 ② The cyber security team at the tech giant—parent of Facebook and Instagram—said it blocked a set of Russia-linked fake accounts that were part of a social media scheme to undermine Ukraine.

③ "They ran websites posing as independent news entities
10 and created fake personas across social media platforms including Facebook, Instagram, Twitter, YouTube, Telegram and also Russian Odnoklassniki and VK," Meta said in a blog post.

④ "In some cases, they used profile pictures that we believe
15 were likely generated using artificial intelligence techniques."

⑤ The small network of Facebook and Instagram accounts targeted people in Ukraine, using posts to try to get people to visit websites featuring bogus news about the country's effort to defend itself from the invasion by Russia.

20 ⑥ Meta said it connected the network to people in Russia and Ukraine, as well as media organizations NewsFront and SouthFront in Crimea.

⑦ The US has identified NewsFront and SouthFront as disinformation outlets that get marching orders from
25 Russian intelligence services.

⑧ The organizations were among more than a dozen entities sanctioned by Washington for trying to influence the 2020 US presidential election at the direction of the leadership of the Russian Government.

30 ⑨ "Meta shut down the bogus accounts and blocked sharing

Pro-Russia
ロシア支持の

Meta
Facebook、Instagram、WhatsApp などのソーシャルアプリを提供する米国の IT 大手企業。旧フェイスブック

blog post
ブログ記事

Crimea
クリミア（黒海の北岸から突き出した半島）

intelligence service
情報機関

Washington
米国政府

of internet addresses involved in the deception," director of threat disruption David Agranovich said in a briefing.

⑩ Bogus claims published by the sites include that the West had betrayed Ukraine and that Ukraine is a failed state, according to Agranovich.

'Ghostwriter'

⑪ Meanwhile, a hacking group called Ghostwriter believed to operate out of Russia has ramped up action against military figures and journalists in Ukraine in recent days, according to Meta's security team.

⑫ Ghostwriter's typical tactic is to target victims with phishing emails that trick them into clicking on deceptive links in an effort to steal log-in credentials.

⑬ The goal of compromising Facebook accounts appeared to be to spread links to misinformation, such as a YouTube video falsely contending to be of Ukrainian soldiers surrendering to Russian troops, according to Meta.

⑭ "We've taken steps to secure accounts that we believe were targeted by this threat actor," said Meta head of security policy Nathaniel Gleicher.

⑮ "We also blocked phishing domains these hackers used to try to trick people in Ukraine into compromising their online accounts."

⑯ Facebook on Friday restricted Russian state media's ability to earn money on the social media platform as Moscow's invasion of neighboring Ukraine reached the streets of Kyiv.

log-in credential
ログイン認証情報

Moscow
ロシア政府（ロシアの首都
があるところから）

While reading 1 次に関して、記事を読んで分かったことをメモしてみましょう。

ロシアと関連する偽アカウントで行われていたこと

....

While reading 2 記事の中で次の情報が述べられている段落の番号を書きましょう。

1. Meta が発表を行った曜日： [　　　　]

2. ロシアの SNS の名前： [　　　　]

3. David Agranovich 氏の地位： [　　　　]

4. Nathaniel Gleicher 氏の地位： [　　　　]

While reading 3 空欄に適切な単語を入れ、記事の要約を完成させましょう。最初の文字がヒントとして示してあります。

On February 27, 2022, the cyber ¹⁾s_____ team at Meta, parent of Facebook and Instagram, said it blocked a set of Russia-linked fake accounts that were part of a social media scheme to ²⁾u_____ Ukraine. They ran websites posing as independent news entities and created fake personas across social media platforms. In some cases, they used ³⁾p_____ pictures that we believe were likely generated using artificial intelligence techniques. Meanwhile, a ⁴⁾h_____ group called Ghostwriter believed to operate out of Russia has ramped up action against military figures and ⁵⁾j_____ in Ukraine in recent days.

While reading 4 3で空欄に入れた単語が正しいか、音声で確認しましょう。

🔊 2-48

While reading 5 記事が示唆する内容と合致すれば T、しなければ F を記入しましょう。

1. Instagram and Facebook are owned by the same company.　[　　　　]

2. VK is a Russian social media platform.　[　　　　]

3. There is evidence to show that some profile pictures were generated using artificial intelligence techniques.　[　　　　]

4. The US sanctioned more than 10 entities which tried to influence the 2020 US presidential election.　[　　　　]

 語句を並べ替えて英文を完成させましょう。間違った場合、解答欄に
正しい答えを書くこと。

1. そのネットワークは、投稿を用いて人々を偽ニュースを報じるウェブサイトに誘導しようとした。

The network used posts to (to / to / get / try / visit / people) websites featuring
bogus news.

予想：..

解答： *The network used posts to*
websites featuring bogus news.

2. 嘘の主張には、西側がウクライナを裏切ったことも含まれている。

Bogus claims (had / that / include / Ukraine / betrayed / the West).

予想：..

解答： *Bogus claims*
....

3. メタは、嘘に関わったネットアドレスの共有を停止した。

Meta (in / of / blocked / sharing / involved / internet addresses) the
deception.

予想：..

解答： *Meta*
the deception.

4. あるハッキンググループはウクライナのジャーナリストに対するアクションを急増させている。

A hacking group (up / has / action / ramped / against / journalists) in
Ukraine.

予想：..

解答： *A hacking group*
in Ukraine.

 次の説明はどの語についてのものか、文中から抜き出して必要に応じ正しい形に直しましょう。最初の文字がヒントとして示してあります。

1. a series of actions intended to achieve a particular result relating to politics or business, or a social improvement

2. someone who is used by a more powerful person or group and has no control of the situation

3. dishonest behavior that is intended to deceive someone

4. the process of choosing a person or a group of people for a position, especially a political position, by voting

5. a meeting in which people are given instructions or information

6. someone who secretly uses or changes the information in other people's computer system

1. c _____	2. p _____	3. d _____
4. e _____	5. b _____	6. h _____

After reading 3 次の課題について、自分の考えを述べましょう。

SNS の偽情報に惑わされないようにするために、どういうことが必要だと思いますか。またそれが必要だと思う理由はなんですか。あなたの考えを書いてみましょう。

日本語でのメモ

英語での作文

96

UNIT 17

Mitsubishi, Mitsui to team up on CO₂ storage project

三菱商事と三井物産、CO₂ 貯留事業で協力へ

昨今の気候変動の原因の一つに、二酸化炭素をはじめとする温室効果ガスの増加があります。この Unit では、三菱商事と三井物産というこれまでライバル関係にあった企業がタッグを組み、海底での二酸化炭素貯留の取り組みを行うことを報じた記事を取り上げます。

🔲 Before reading 1

説明を読み、内容に関する理解を深めましょう。
また図からどんなことが言えるか考えましょう。

- 政 府 は 2050 年までに二酸化炭素（carbon dioxide）の 排 出（emission）を 実 質 ゼ ロ（net-zero）にする脱炭素（decarbonization）を目標に掲げています。

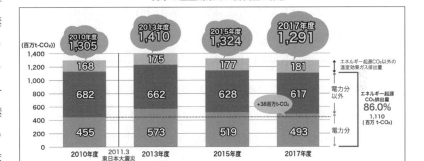

日本の温室効果ガス排出量の推移

出典：資源エネルギー庁ウェブサイト
(https://www.enecho.meti.go.jp/about/pamphlet/energy2019/html/003/)

- 脱炭素の実現には、二酸化炭素を回収して地下にためる CCS（Carbon Capture and Storage）の技術が重要と考えられています。

🔲 Before reading 2

日本語に対応する英語表現を選択肢から選び、○で囲みましょう。

1. 水素　　　　　　　　oxygen / hydrogen

2. 火力　　　　　　　　thermal power / plu-thermal power

3. 再生可能エネルギー　　renewable energy / returnable energy

4. 合弁事業　　　　　　joint venture / joined venture

5. 経済産業省　　　　　the Economy, Trade and Industry Ministry /
　　　　　　　　　　　the Economy, Industry and Trade Ministry

Mitsubishi, Mitsui to team up on CO₂ storage project

① Mitsubishi Corp. and Mitsui & Co. plan to launch a project to store carbon dioxide in the seabed off Western Australia, The Yomiuri Shimbun has learned.

② The rival companies are joining forces for the so-called Carbon Capture and Storage (CCS) project, in which CO₂ is captured and then stored under the ocean.

③ This technology has attracted attention as a way to promote decarbonization, and Mitsubishi and Mitsui envisage handling CO₂ emissions from Japanese companies in the future, according to sources.

④ They plan to begin by March procedures to obtain permission from the Australian government to conduct a detailed survey of the ocean floor, the sources said.

⑤ The sea area off Western Australia, where the project is planned to take place, has the highest concentration of offshore gas fields in Australia. A large amount of natural gas has been produced in the area, and hopes are high that a large amount of CO₂ can be stored in the gaps where the gas used to be.

⑥ Mitsubishi and Mitsui have already started extracting natural gas in the area through a joint venture, so they have a certain level of expertise regarding the seabed layers in the area.

⑦ Major resources companies BP PLC of Britain and Woodside Petroleum Ltd. of Australia are also expected to participate, and the total investment will reach several

提供 : Science Photo Library / アフロ
Mitsubishi Corp.
三菱商事株式会社
Mitsui & Co.
三井物産株式会社

Carbon Capture and Storage　二酸化炭素回収貯留

ocean floor　海洋底

BP PLC　イギリスの大手石油会社で、国際石油資本（メジャーズ）の一つ。
Woodside Petroleum Ltd. 石油調査・製造の会社で、オーストラリアのエネルギー大手。

hundred billion yen.

⑧ Facilities for the CCS project are expected to go into operation around 2030, according to the sources.

⑨ Initially, CO_2 emitted by local factories will be taken in through a pipeline. At a later time, CO_2 emitted by Japanese companies, such as those in the steel, chemicals and shipping industries, will be transported by sea and stored in the seabed.

⑩ Compared to Europe and elsewhere, Japan has fewer areas suitable for generating solar power and other forms of renewable energy.

⑪ As a certain amount of thermal power generation may continue to be necessary, the CCS technology has been regarded as important to achieve carbon neutrality, or net-zero CO_2 emissions.

carbon neutrality
炭素中立

⑫ The technology is also expected to be used to offset CO_2 emitted during the production of hydrogen and ammonia, which have drawn attention as next-generation fuels that will support decarbonization.

offset　相殺する

⑬ However, there are many challenges involved, as a business model for capturing and storing CO_2 has not been established yet. Mitsubishi and Mitsui will accelerate their efforts to reduce the cost of capturing and transporting CO_2, among other costs.

⑭ The Economy, Trade and Industry Ministry is working to create international rules to allow companies to trade the CO_2 emissions that they reduce with the use of the CCS technology.

 **While reading 1** 次に関して、記事を読んで分かったことをメモしてみましょう。

CCS 技術及びこの技術によって期待されること

記事の中で次の情報が述べられている段落の番号を書きましょう。

1. 三菱商事と三井物産がオーストラリア政府からの許可取得手続きを始める時期： [   ]

2. 三菱商事と三井物産以外に参加を予定している企業： [   ]

3. CCS 事業の施設が稼働を予定している時期： [   ]

4. 経済産業省が取り組んでいること： [   ]

While reading 3   空欄に適切な単語または数字を入れ、記事の要約を完成させましょう。
答えが単語の場合、最初の文字がヒントとして示してあります。

Compared to Europe and elsewhere, Japan has fewer areas suitable for generating $^{1)}$s_____ power and other forms of renewable energy. Thus, a certain amount of $^{2)}$t_____ power generation may continue to be necessary. In order to achieve carbon $^{3)}$n_____, Mitsubishi Corp. and Mitsui & Co. plan to launch a project to store carbon dioxide in the $^{4)}$s_____ off Western Australia. They plan to begin by March procedures to obtain permission from the Australian government. Facilities for the CCS project are expected to go into operation around $^{5)}$_____.

While reading 4   3で空欄に入れた単語または数字が正しいか、音声で確認しましょう。

🔊 2-56

While reading 5   記事が示唆する内容と合致すれば T、しなければ F を記入しましょう。

1. Mitsubishi Corp. has no special knowledge or skills regarding the seabed layers in the sea area off Western Australia.   [   ]

2. It will take at least more than 10 years before facilities for the CCS project go into operation.   [   ]

3. More areas are available for generating solar power in Europe than in Japan.   [   ]

4. Due to geographical reasons, it is difficult for Japan to completely stop using thermal power.   [   ]

 **After reading 1** 語句を並べ替えて英文を完成させましょう。間違った場合、解答欄に正しい答えを書くこと。

1. 水素とアンモニアは脱炭素を支援する次世代の燃料として注目を集めてきた。

Hydrogen and ammonia (as / have / that / drawn / attention / next-generation fuels) will support decarbonization.

予想：......

解答： *Hydrogen and ammonia* ......
will support decarbonization.

2. その事業はオーストラリア西部沖合の海底で行われる計画だ。

The project (in / is / to / take / place / planned) the seabed off Western Australia.

予想：......

解答： *The project* ...... *the*
seabed off Western Australia.

3. その2つの会社はオーストラリア政府から許可を得るための手続きを開始するつもりだ。

The two companies (to / to / plan / begin / obtain / procedures) permission from the Australian government.

予想：......

解答： *The two companies* ......
permission from the Australian government.

4. 日本企業が排出した二酸化炭素は海路で運ばれることになるだろう。

CO2 (be / by / will / emitted / transported / Japanese companies) by sea.

予想：......

解答： *CO2* ......
by sea.

 **After reading 2** 次の説明はどの語についてのものか、文中から抜き出して必要に応じ正しい形に直しましょう。最初の文字がヒントとして示してあります。

1. a chemical substance that exists in a pure form as diamonds, graphite, etc., or in an impure form as coal, petrol, etc.

2. a person, group, or organization that you compete with in sport, business, a fight, etc.

3. to think something is likely to happen in the future

4. in or under the sea and not far from the coast

5. special skills or knowledge in a particular subject, that you learn by experience or training

6. a colorless gas that is the lightest of all gases, forms water when it combines with oxygen, and is used to produce ammonia and other chemicals

1. c _____	2. r _____	3. e _____
4. o _____	5. e _____	6. h _____

After reading 3 次の課題について、自分の考えを述べましょう。

二酸化炭素の排出を抑えるために、私たちは普段の生活で何ができるでしょうか。またそれを行うためにどんなことを意識すればよいでしょうか。あなたの考えを書いてみましょう。

日本語でのメモ

英語での作文

UNIT 18

Airlines search for new profit streams

航空会社、新たな収益の流れを探索

新型コロナウイルスの感染拡大の影響を大きく受けた業界の一つが航空業界です。特に、国際線の利用客はコロナ下で大幅な減少が続いています。この **Unit** では、航空会社が収益を確保しようと事業構造の転換に取り組んでいることを報じた記事を取り上げます。

⊞ Before reading 1

説明を読み、内容に関する理解を深めましょう。
また図からどんなことが言えるか考えましょう。

- 新型コロナウイルスのパンデミックの影響により、国際線（international flight）の乗客（passenger）数は大きく減少（plunge）し、年末年始を除く国内線（domestic flight）の乗客数もパンデミック前（pre-pandemic）の半分以下になっています。

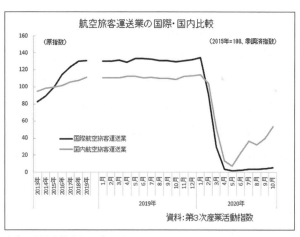

出典：経済産業省ウェブサイト
(https://www.meti.go.jp/statistics/toppage/report/minikaisetsu/
hitokoto_kako/20201223hitokoto.html)

⊞ Before reading 2   日本語に対応する英語表現を選択肢から選び、○で囲みましょう。

1. 変異株　　　　　　　　varier / variant

2. 地域の特産品　　　　　local specialty / local spatiality

3. 機内食　　　　　　　　in-flight meal / off-flight meal

4. 人件費　　　　　　　　personal expenses / personnel expenses

5. 純損失、最終赤字　　　net loss / total loss

Airlines search for new profit streams

写真：AFP/WAA

① With their flight operations suffering losses amid the pandemic, airlines are finding creative ways to branch into new businesses or wring the last drops of value out of retiring aircraft.

② With the omicron variant of the novel coronavirus compounding their worries, airlines are at a crucial juncture.
③ This month, Japan Airlines was set to launch a business to assist Japanese companies in marketing their goods online to consumers in China. Using an exclusive page of the WeChat communication app from leading Chinese IT firm Tencent, JAL will help Japanese companies promote, sell and deliver their products. The airline will also support the tasks of collecting and delivering local specialties from around Japan.

④ ANA Holdings Inc. last autumn began selling interior equipment from its aircraft through an online auction run by Yahoo Japan Corp. Items put up for sale included seats of the type used in first class on international flights, which normally would have been discarded when no longer needed, and window frames of large aircraft.

⑤ Both JAL and ANA have also begun to sell their in-flight meals on the ground. Previously, they had sold such instant foods as cup noodles, but now both have upgraded their offerings to include frozen in-flight meals, which have become hit products.

⑥ The airline industry remains in an enervated state, with

omicron variant
オミクロン株

Japan Airlines
日本航空株式会社

WeChat　微信
（ウィーチャット）
Tencent　テンセント
JAL　Japan Airlines の略
称

ANA Holdings Inc.
ANA ホールディングス株
式会社

Yahoo Japan Corp.
ヤフー株式会社

passenger numbers on international flights yet to recover from a 90% plunge from pre-pandemic levels. Even domestic flights tend to be less than half full, although the New Year holiday period has been an exception.

35 ⑦ Both airlines are expected to log a net loss on their consolidated statements for the fiscal year ending on March 31, marking a second consecutive annual loss. The awaited upturn in their performance has been slower than expected.

40 ⑧ Both have been striving to streamline their operations at a fast pace. Both have reduced their personnel expenses by loaning their employees to other companies and cutting bonuses while reviewing the number of flights they operate. "We've been trying out all possibilities," a senior official of 45 ANA Holdings said.

⑨ They have also been exploring new ways to make use of their aircraft. For a limited period, ANA offered a Boeing 777 that was set to be retired from service for use as a wedding hall. A couple could hold a reception on 50 board, with a cabin attendant giving her blessing to the newlyweds as an in-flight announcement. The company has been pushing ahead with retiring its larger, less fuel-efficient aircraft as part of its structural reforms, but this service was proposed by an employee so that such aircraft 55 can make one last contribution to the company's earnings, no matter how small.

New Year holiday period　年末年始の時期

consolidated statement
連結財務諸表

senior official　幹部社員

newlywed　新婚夫婦

push ahead with ～
～を押し進める

 **While reading** 次に関して、記事を読んで分かったことをメモしてみましょう。

1. JAL の取り組み

....

2. ANA の取り組み

....

1. 中国の IT 大手企業の名前： [   ]

2. ANA が機内備品の売却に利用したネットオークションを運営する会社の名前： [   ]

3. パンデミック前と比較した国際線の乗客数の減少割合： [   ]

4. ANA 幹部の発言： [   ]

While reading 3 空欄に適切な単語または数字を入れ、記事の要約を完成させましょう。答えが単語の場合、最初の文字がヒントとして示してあります。

The airline ¹⁾i＿＿＿＿＿＿＿ remains in an enervated state, with passenger numbers on international flights yet to recover from a ²⁾＿＿＿＿% plunge from pre-pandemic levels. Under such circumstances, both JAL and ANA have been striving to ³⁾s＿＿＿＿＿＿ their operations at a fast pace. Both have reduced their personnel expenses by loaning their employees to other companies and cutting ⁴⁾b＿＿＿＿＿＿ while reviewing the number of flights they operate. In addition, these airlines are finding creative ways to branch into new businesses or wring the last drops of value out of ⁵⁾r＿＿＿＿＿＿ aircraft.

While reading 4 3 で空欄に入れた単語または数字が正しいか、音声で確認しましょう。

🔊 2-62

While reading 5 記事が示唆する内容と合致すれば T、しなければ F を記入しましょう。

1. ANA Holdings Inc. started selling interior equipment from its aircraft through an online auction from the fall of 2022.   [   ]

2. Passenger numbers on international flights decreased to less than a quarter from pre-pandemic levels.   [   ]

3. During the New Year period, many domestic flights are more than half full.   [   ]

4. JAL recorded an annual loss in fiscal 2020.   [   ]

 **After reading 1** 語句を並べ替えて英文を完成させましょう。間違った場合、解答欄に正しい答えを書くこと。

1. JAL と ANA の両社は、自社の飛行機を活用する新たな方法を模索している。

Both JAL and ANA have (to / use / been / make / exploring / new ways) of their aircraft.

予 想：..

....

解 答：*Both JAL and ANA have*

                                    of their aircraft.

....

2. その航空会社は日本中の地域特産品の配達業務を支援する予定だ。

The airline (of / will / support / delivering / the task / local specialties) from around Japan.

予 想：..

....

解 答：*The airline*

                              from around Japan.

....

3. その飛行機は退役が予定されていた。

The aircraft was (be / to / set / from / retired / service).

予 想：..

解 答：*The aircraft was*

....

4. 国際線のファーストクラスで使われた座席は必要がなくなると捨てられてきた。

Seats used in first class on international flights (been / have / when / would / discarded / no longer) needed.

予 想：..

....

解 答：*Seats used in first class on international flights*

                                    needed.

....

 **After reading 2** 次の説明はどの語についてのものか、文中から抜き出して必要に応じ正しい形に直しましょう。最初の文字がヒントとして示してあります。

1. a disease that affects people over a very large area or the whole world

2. to succeed in getting something from someone, but only after a lot of effort

3. to improve something and make it more modern, especially in order to provide a better service

4. something or someone that is not included in a general statement or does not follow a rule or pattern

5. to make something such as a business, organization, etc., work more simply and effectively

6. a large formal party to celebrate an event or to welcome someone

1. p＿＿＿＿＿	2. w＿＿＿＿＿	3. u＿＿＿＿＿
4. e＿＿＿＿＿	5. s＿＿＿＿＿	6. r＿＿＿＿＿

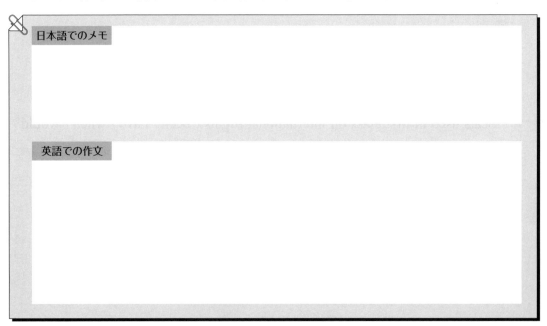 **After reading 3** 次の課題について、自分の考えを述べましょう。

パンデミックの影響を受けた産業を支援するために、どのような取り組みが必要だと思いますか。またその取り組みが必要だと思う理由は何ですか。あなたの考えを書いてみましょう。

日本語でのメモ

英語での作文

UNIT 19

Germany to close nuclear reactors despite energy crisis

ドイツ、エネルギー危機も原子炉を閉鎖へ

ドイツは環境に対する意識が高く、再生可能エネルギーの活用に熱心に取り組んでいます。この Unit では、エネルギー価格が上昇を続ける中でも、ドイツが原発を閉鎖し、再生可能エネルギーへの転換を進めることを報じた記事を紹介します。

🔂 Before reading 1

説明を読み、内容に関する理解を深めましょう。
また図からどんなことが言えるか考えましょう。

- ドイツ（Germany）における原子力（atomic energy）の利用は 2011 年の福島原発事故（nuclear disaster）を契機に見直しが進み、メルケル前首相は 2022 年末までに廃止する（abandon）ことを決定していました。

- 原子力（nuclear power）発電は化石燃料を用いず、二酸化炭素を排出しない点で再生可能エネルギー（renewable energy）と共通します。

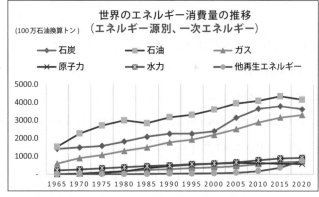

出典：「世界のエネルギー消費量の推移」（資源エネルギー庁）
(https://www.enecho.meti.go.jp/about/whitepaper/2022/html/2-2-1.html) を元に作成

🔂 Before reading 2

日本語に対応する英語表現を選択肢から選び、〇で囲みましょう。

1. 移行　　　　　　　　　　transition / transaction

2. 達成、実現　　　　　　　fruition / fragmentation

3. 化石燃料　　　　　　　　fossil fuel / synthetic fuel

4. （独、オーストリア）首相　chancellor / key minister

5. 地政学的緊張　　　　　　geological tension / geopolitical tension

Germany to close nuclear reactors despite energy crisis

① Germany shut down three nuclear power plants on Friday even as Europe faces one of its worst ever energy crises, following Angela Merkel's timetable for phasing out atomic energy.

② With energy prices already on the rise and tensions higher than ever between Europe and key gas supplier Russia, the closure of the plants in Brokdorf, Grohnde and Gundremmingen could well tighten the squeeze.

③ The move halved remaining nuclear capacity in Germany and reduced energy output by around four gigawatts—equivalent to the power produced by 1,000 wind turbines.

④ Protests over the Fukushima nuclear disaster in 2011 prompted former chancellor Merkel to set the wheels in motion for abandoning nuclear power just over 10 years ago.

⑤ Germany is planning to completely wind down atomic energy by the end of 2022, when it will shut its final three plants in Neckarwestheim, Essenbach and Emsland.

⑥ But with energy prices soaring across Europe, the timing of the plans coming to fruition could hardly be worse.

⑦ Europe's reference gas price, Dutch TTF, hit 187.78 euros per megawatt hour in December—10 times higher than at the start of last year—and electricity prices are also soaring.

⑧ The spike has been fuelled by geopolitical tensions with Russia, which supplies one third of Europe's gas.

⑨ Western countries accuse Russia of limiting gas deliveries to put pressure on Europe amid tensions over the Ukraine conflict.

⑩ Moscow also wants to push through the controversial Nord Stream 2 pipeline, set to ship still more Russian gas to Germany.

Glossary

nuclear power plant 原子力発電所
Angela Merkel アンゲラ・メルケル
phase out ～ ～を段階的に廃止する
Brokdorf ブロクドルフ
Grohnde グローンデ
Gundremmingen グンドレンミンゲン
set the wheels in motion 事を実行に移す、行動にかかる
wind down ～ ～を段階的に縮小する
Neckarwestheim ネッカーヴェストハイム
Essenbach エッセンバッハ
Emsland エムスラント
reference 基準の
gas delivery ガスの供給
set to ～ ～へ向かう
ship ～ ～を送る

Price hikes

⑪ The end of nuclear power in Germany will likely push prices up even further, according to Sebastian Herold, a professor of energy policy at the Darmstadt University of Applied Sciences.

⑫ "In the long term, the hope is that an increase in renewable energy will balance things out, but this will not be the case in the short term," he told AFP.

⑬ Until Germany can really ramp up renewables, it will remain dependent on fossil fuels to plug the gap left by the nuclear exit.

⑭ "This will make Germany more dependent on natural gas overall, at least in the short term, and thus also a little more dependent on Russia," Herold said.

⑮ The transition may also take longer than Germany would like, with progress on renewables slowed in recent years by opposition to energy infrastructure projects.

⑯ The proportion of energy generated by renewables is expected to fall in 2021 for the first time since 1997 to 42 percent, compared with 45.3 percent in 2020.

⑰ As well as driving up prices, the nuclear plant closures will also remove a key source of low-carbon energy in a country that is already struggling to meet ambitious climate goals.

Darmstadt University of Applied Sciences ダルムシュタット工科大学

balance things out 物事のバランスをとる、帳尻合わせをする

opposition to ～ ～との対照で

drive up ～ ～を押し上げる
low-carbon 低炭素

 **While reading 1** 次に関して、記事を読んで分かったことをメモしてみましょう。

ドイツの原発全廃計画

While reading 2 記事の中で次の情報が述べられている段落の番号を書きましょう。

1. 福島で原発事故が発生した年：[　　　]

2. 2022 年末までに閉鎖される予定の原発がある場所：[　　　]

3. 2021 年 12 月時点でのヨーロッパの 1 メガワットあたりの標準ガス価格：[　　　]

4. 2021 年に再生可能エネルギーが（エネルギー全体に対して）占める割合：[　　　]

While reading 3 空欄に適切な単語または数字を入れ、記事の要約を完成させましょう。答えが単語の場合、最初の文字がヒントとして示してあります。

Following Angela Merkel's ¹⁾t_____ for phasing out atomic energy, Germany shut down three nuclear power plants on December 31, 2021, even as Europe faces one of its worst ever energy ²⁾c_____. The move halved remaining nuclear capacity in the country and reduced energy ³⁾o_____ by around four gigawatts. Germany is planning to completely wind down atomic energy by the end of ⁴⁾_____, when it will shut its final three plants in Neckarwestheim, Essenbach and Emsland. But with energy prices soaring across Europe, the timing of the plans coming to ⁵⁾f_____ could hardly be worse.

While reading 4 3 で空欄に入れた単語または数字が正しいか、音声で確認しましょう。

🔊 2-72

While reading 5 記事が示唆する内容と合致すれば T、しなければ F を記入しましょう。

1. One wind turbine produces around four megawatts on average. [　　　]

2. Europe's reference gas price was less than 20 euros per megawatt hour in January, 2021. [　　　]

3. Some people do not support Nord Stream 2. [　　　]

4. Compared to 2020, the proportion of renewable energy is expected to fall by more than five percent in 2021. [　　　]

 **After reading 1** 　語句を並べ替えて英文を完成させましょう。間違った場合、解答欄に正しい答えを書くこと。

1. その抗議は前首相に対して原子力の廃止を実行するよう促した。

The protests (in / to / set / prompted / the wheels / the former chancellor) motion for abandoning nuclear power.

予想：
....

解答： *The protests*
　　　　　　　　　　　　　motion for abandoning nuclear power.

2. 原子力からの撤退は、ドイツをよりロシアに依存させることになるだろう。

The nuclear exit (on / will / make / Russia / Germany / more dependent).

予想：
....

解答： *The nuclear exit*
....

3. 昨年 12 月のヨーロッパの基準ガス価格は昨年の始めより 10 倍高かった。

Europe's reference gas price last December was (at / of / than / higher / 10 times / the start) last year.

予想：
....

解答： *Europe's reference gas price was*
　　　　　　　　　　　　　　　　last year.

4. 教授は AFP に対し、帳尻合わせは短期的には該当しないと述べた。

The professor told AFP that balancing things out (be / in / not / would / the case / the short term).

予想：
....

解答： *The professor told AFP that balancing things out*
....

113

1. the feeling that exists when people or countries do not trust each other and may suddenly attack each other or start arguing

2. an engine or motor in which the pressure of a liquid or gas moves a special wheel around

3. the successful result of a plan, a process or an activity

4. causing a lot of disagreement, because many people have strong opinions about the subject being discussed

5. the process or a period of changing from one state or condition to another

6. needing a lot of effort, money or time to succeed

1. t _____	2. t _____	3. f _____
4. c _____	5. t _____	6. a _____

After reading 3 次の課題について、自分の考えを述べましょう。

あなたは日本の原発を廃止すべきだと思いますか。また廃止すべき／廃止すべきでないと思う理由はなんですか。あなたの考えを書いてみましょう。

日本語でのメモ

英語での作文

UNIT 20

Health first, freedom second? How Covid is changing democracies

健康第一、自由は第二？ コロナは民主主義をどう変えつつある

新型コロナウイルスのパンデミックによって、人々はロックダウンを始め、様々な行動の制限を強いられました。この Unit では、そのような行動の制限が民主主義にどのような影響を与えたかを報じた記事を紹介します。

Before reading 1

説明を読み、内容に関する理解を深めましょう。
また図からどんなことが言えるか考えましょう。

- 新型コロナウイルスのパンデミック (pandemic) によって、ロックダウン (lockdown) やマスク着用義務化 (mandatory mask-wearing)、娯楽・スポーツ施設 (entertainment and sporting venue) 利用時の接種証明書 (Covid pass) など、市民的自由に対する様々な制限 (restriction) が課されるようになりました。

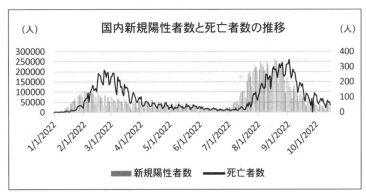

国内新規陽性者数と死亡者数の推移

出典：「データからわかる－新型コロナウイルス感染症情報－」（厚生労働省）より作成
(https://covid19.mhlw.go.jp/)

Before reading 2

日本語に対応する英語表現を選択肢から選び、○で囲みましょう。

1. 迫害　　　　　　　　persecution　/　prosecution

2. 騒動　　　　　　　　fury　/　furor

3. 監視機関　　　　　　watchdog　/　watcheye

4. 夜間外出禁止令　　　curfew　/　curb line

5. 市民的自由　　　　　civil liberty　/　civil liberticide

Health first, freedom second? How Covid is changing democracies

① From a litany of lockdowns to mandatory mask-wearing and Covid passes to access entertainment and sporting venues, the pandemic has led to sweeping restrictions on civil liberties in some of the world's oldest democracies.

5 ② Among Western countries, European nations particularly have been quick to crimp basic freedoms in the name of fighting the virus.

③ French President Emmanuel Macron caused a furor this week by saying he wanted to piss off those who refuse to get 10 vaccinated by limiting as much as possible their access to activities in social life.

④ The remarks from the leader of a country that sees itself as a global beacon of liberty underscore the extent to which the pandemic has changed national priorities.

15 ⑤ The United States has also taken aggressive steps, including closing its borders to most of the world for 20 months and making vaccinations mandatory for all federal employees and staff of big companies.

⑥ The Berlin-based rights watchdog Civil Liberties Union for 20 Europe warned in a report last year that measures targeting the unvaccinated could exacerbate existing inequalities.

⑦ "(They) may create a two-tier society where some people may enjoy an extensive set of freedoms and rights while others are excluded," the report said.

25

Persecution or protection?

⑧ At the start of the pandemic, governments used sweeping lockdowns and curfews to try to contain the virus.

⑨ But in the past year, most countries began refining their 30 strategies, rolling out digital passes allowing people to show

a litany of 〜	(うんざりする程) 多くの〜
democracies	民主主義国
Emmanuel Macron	エマニュエル・マクロン氏
piss off 〜	〜をいらいらさせる、うんざりさせる
Civil Liberties Union for Europe	欧州自由人権協会
two-tier	二層の
contain	封じ込める
roll out 〜	〜を始める

they are vaccinated.

⑩ Faced with the Omicron variant, some governments, notably Austria and the Netherlands, reverted to one-size-fits-all tactics and ordered people back indoors during the end-of-year celebrations.

⑪ But worldwide, many countries are now turning the screws on citizens who are refusing to be jabbed.

⑫ Austria kept the unvaccinated confined to their homes last month after lifting a partial lockdown. In February, the country will be the first in Europe to make vaccines compulsory for most people.

⑬ British Prime Minister Boris Johnson says his country also needs to have a national conversation about mandatory vaccinations, echoing similar comments from the German government.

⑭ The French government meanwhile has proposed to follow Germany's lead by barring the unvaccinated from restaurants, cinemas and leisure facilities.

⑮ While public acceptance of Covid restrictions was high at the outset of the crisis, pandemic fatigue is fueling growing resistance to new curbs.

⑯ The unvaccinated complain of discrimination, with some going so far as to compare their treatment to the persecution of European Jews during World War II.

⑰ And from the Netherlands to Austria, Germany, Belgium and France, thousands of people have taken to the streets—sometimes clashing with police—to protest Covid rules and health passes.

Glossary
Omicron variant オミクロン変異株
one-size-fits-all 画一的な
turn the screws on ~ ~への圧迫を一層加える
Boris Johnson ボリス・ジョンソン氏
echo ~ ~を真似する
bar ~ ~を締め出す
at the outset of ~ ~の始まりで
so far as to ~ ~するところまで

 **While reading 1** 次に関して、記事を読んで分かったことをメモしてみましょう。

米国のコロナ対策

While reading 2

記事の中で次の情報が述べられている段落の番号を書きましょう。

1. フランス大統領の名前：[　　　　]

2. Civil Liberties Union for Europe の本拠地がある都市：[　　　　]

3. ワクチンの義務化を予定している欧州で最初の国：[　　　　]

4. ワクチン非接種者に対する扱いで比較対象とされた人々：[　　　　]

While reading 3

空欄に適切な単語を入れ、記事の要約を完成させましょう。
最初の文字がヒントとして示してあります。

From a litany of lockdowns to mandatory mask-wearing and Covid
1)p_____ to access entertainment and sporting venues, the pandemic has
led to sweeping restrictions on 2)c_____ liberties in some of the world's
oldest democracies, particularly European nations. The Berlin-based rights
3)w_____ Civil Liberties Union for Europe warned in a 2021 report that
measures targeting the unvaccinated could exacerbate existing 4)i_____.
The unvaccinated complain of discrimination, with some going so far as to
compare their treatment to the 5)p_____ of European Jews during World
War II.

While reading 4

3で空欄に入れた単語が正しいか、音声で確認しましょう。

🔊 2-82

While reading 5

記事が示唆する内容と合致すれば T、しなければ F を記入しましょう。

1. Civil liberties in European nations were more respected before the pandemic.
[　　　]

2. The United States decided to limit the entry of people from most of the world
from the start of 2021.　[　　　]

3. The Netherlands ordered its people to stay home at the start of the pandemic.
[　　　]

4. When the pandemic started, there was more resistance to Covid restrictions
among European people than now.　[　　　]

語句を並べ替えて英文を完成させましょう。間違った場合、解答欄に正しい答えを書くこと。

1. マクロン大統領はワクチン接種を拒む人々をうんざりさせることを望んだ。

President Macron wanted to piss (to / get / off / who / those / refuse) vaccinated.

予想：

解答： *President Macron wanted to piss*
　　　　　　　　vaccinated.

2. 政府はワクチン未接種者を娯楽施設から締め出す提案を行った。

The government (to / bar / from / proposed / the unvaccinated / leisure facilities).

予想：

解答： *The government*

3. 米国は大企業の社員のワクチン接種を義務化した。

The United States (of / for / made / staff / mandatory / vaccinations) big companies.

予想：

解答： *The United States*
　　　　　　　big companies.

4. 数千人もの人々が通りに出てコロナの規制への抗議を行った。

Thousands of people (to / to / took / protest / the streets / Covid rules).

予想：

解答： *Thousands of people*

次の説明はどの語についてのものか、文中から抜き出して必要に応じ正しい形に直しましょう。最初の文字がヒントとして示してあります。

1. an official piece of paper which shows that you are allowed to enter a building or travel on something without paying

2. a place where an organized meeting, concert, etc., takes place

3. a sudden expression of anger among a large group of people about something that has happened

4. a person or group of people whose job is to protect the rights of people who buy things and to make sure companies do not do anything illegal or harmful

5. a law that forces people to stay indoors after a particular time at night, or the time people must be indoors

6. cruel or unfair treatment of someone over a period of time, especially because of their religious or political beliefs

1. p_____	2. v_____	3. f_____
4. w_____	5. c_____	6. p_____

After reading 3 次の課題について、自分の考えを述べましょう。

もしあなたが政治家だったら、感染対策と権利の保護のどちらを優先しますか。またそれを優先する理由は何ですか。あなたの考えを書いてみましょう。

日本語でのメモ

英語での作文

英字新聞の見出しによく使われる単語

a	**accord**	名	協定、合意、一致 agreement, consent
	act	名	行為、動き activity, movement
	aid	名	援助 assistance
		動	援助する assist, help
	aim	名	目的、狙い purpose, object
		動	目的とする target
	air	動	発表する、表明する、意見を出す announce, voice
	assail	動	攻撃する、非難する attack, criticize
b	**back**	動	支援する support
	bag	動	捕らえる、手に入れる catch
	ban	名	禁止 prohibition
		動	禁じる forbid, prohibit
	bar	動	妨げる, 遮る refuse, shut out
	bid	名	企て、努力、提案 attempt, proposal
		動	要請する order
	blast	名	爆発、爆破 explosion
	blaze	名	火炎、火災 bright fire
	boost	動	(値段などを)押し上げる lift
	brief	動	要点を報告する sum up
c	**charge**	名	告訴 accusation
		動	とがめる、告訴する blame, accuse
	check	動	調査する examine
	cheer	動	声援する encourage
	cite	動	引用する quote
	claim	動	主張する demand
	clash	名	衝突 collision
	confab	名	会議 conference
	confer	動	会談する、協議する consult
	cop	名	警官 policeman
	crash	名	衝突、墜落 conflict, collision
	curb	名	制限、抑制 restraint
		動	拘束する、抑制する check
d	**deal**	名	取引、契約 arrangement, contract
	dip	動	(株価などが)少し下がる come down
	drive	名	運動 campaign
	due	名	予定 schedule

e	**eye**	動	目指す、もくろむ intend, hope
f	**face**	動	直面する confront
	fete	名	祝祭日 festival day
	fire	動	解雇する dismiss
	foil	動	挫折させる baffle
g	**gain**	名	利益、伸び、増進 increase, advance
		動	増加する increase
	grab	動	ひったくる、逮捕する clutch, arrest
	grill	動	厳しく尋問する question severely
h	**hail**	動	歓迎する、賞賛する acclaim, praise
	halt	名	停止 stoppage, suspension
		動	停止させる stop
	head	動	率いる、先頭に立つ、～に向かう lead, precede
	hike	名	値上げ、上昇 increase, raise
		動	(価格を)上げる raise, lift
	hit	動	攻撃する、非難する attack, criticize
	hold	動	拘留する detain, take someone into custody
	hurt	動	傷つける injure, wound
i	**ink**	動	調印する sign a note, affix one's signature
	ire	名	怒り、憤怒 wrath, anger
	issue	名	論争 argument
l	**lash**	動	非難する attack, blame
	laud	動	称賛する praise
	launch	動	始める、着手する start, set about
	list	名	表 table
		動	名簿に記入する set forth
m	**mar**	動	損なう、傷つける damage
	mart	名	市場 market
	meet	名	会議、会合 assembly, meeting
		動	出会う encounter
	mishap	名	事故、災難 accident, disaster

	move	名	処置、行動、運動 movement
		動	動く turn
	mull	動	熟考する ponder
n	nab	動	ひったくる、逮捕する snatch, arrest
	name	動	指名する designate
	near	動	近付く approach
	net	動	捕える trap, snare
	nip	動	阻む、くじく block
	nix	動	否認する、不可とする disapprove
	note	名	公式文書 formal document
		動	気がつく、認める notice, perceive
	nuke	名	核兵器 nuclear arms
o	OK	動	承認する approve
	oust	動	追い出す expel
p	pact	名	条約、協定 treaty, agreement
	parley	名	協議、会談 discussion, conference
	peril	名	危険、危難 danger, hazard
		動	危険にさらす expose to danger
	pick	動	選ぶ choose
	plan	名	計画 project
	plea	名	嘆願 entreaty
	pledge	名	誓約 promise
		動	約束する、誓約する promise
	plot	名	陰謀 conspiracy
		動	陰謀を企てる conspire
	plunge	動	急落する drop (fall) suddenly
	poll	名	投票、世論調査 voting
	post	名	地位 position, station
	prexy	名	大学の学長 president
	probe	名	調査 investigation
		動	調査する investigate
	push	動	押し進める press, impel, drive
q	quake	名	地震 earthquake
	quell	動	鎮圧する suppress
	quit	動	辞める、去る give up, stop, leave
	quiz	名	質問 question
		動	質問する question, interrogate

r	rage	動	猛威を振るう be furious, be violent
	raid	名	侵略、急襲、手入れ attack
		動	襲撃する attack, assault
	rap	名	非難、叱責 censure, reproof
		動	非難する rebuke, blame, censure
	rift	名	割れ目、不和 discord, trouble
	rite	名	儀式 ceremony
	rock	動	激しく揺さぶる shake hard
	rout	動	大勝する win big, get an enemy on the run
	row	名	口論、不和、論争 quarrel
	rule	動	支配する govern, control
	rush	動	急ぐ speed, hasten, hurry up
s	score	動	扱き下ろす、非難する abuse (criticize) severely
	scrap	動	捨てる、廃棄する abandon, do away with, discard
	set	動	着手する、開始する set about, commence, decide
	slam	動	酷評する、非難する denounce
	slap	動	非難する reproach, rebuke
	slash	動	削除する eliminate, delete
	slate	動	予定する schedule
	slay	動	殺害する、惨殺する kill, slaughter
	snag	動	邪魔する、妨害する impede
	snub	動	無視する、はね付ける ignore, rebuff
	solon	名	米国の上院議員、下院議員 senator, representative or congressman
	split	名	分裂 division
		動	分裂する be disunited, be torn
	stab	動	刺す pierce, thrust
	stage	動	行う、計画する carry out
	stall	動	行き詰まる come to a standstill
	stem	動	食い止める、押える dam up, stop, check
	stir	動	動かす move, touch, inspire
	stress	動	強調する emphasize
	sue	動	訴える claim, tale to court
	suit	名	訴訟 lawsuit
	swap	名	交換 exchange
		動	交換する、交易する trade, exchange

t	talks	名	会談 negotiations
	test	名	検査、実験 experiment, trial
		動	実験する、試験する examine
	tie	名	関係 relation
	toll	名	代償、犠牲、死者数 fatalities, casual-ties
	tremor	名	地震 temblor, earthquake
	trim	動	削減する reduce, cut down
u	**up**	動	増大する、昇進させる increase, promote
	urge	動	要請する request, ask
v	**vex**	動	悩ます bother, worry, torment
	vie	動	競う、張り合う compete, contend
	vow	動	誓う swear
w	**wed**	動	結婚する marry, get married to
	win	名	勝利 victory
		動	打ち勝つ beat, defeat

新聞・雑誌によく出る略語

ADB	Asian Development Bank アジア開発銀行
AIDS	acquired immune deficiency syndrome 後天性免疫不全症候群、エイズ
ANA	All Nippon Airways 全日本空輸株式会社（全日空）
APEC	Asia-Pacific Economic Cooperation アジア太平洋経済協力
ASEAN	Association of Southeast Asian Nations 東南アジア諸国連合
BOJ	Bank of Japan 日本銀行
CEO	chief executive officer 最高経営責任者
CIA	Central Intelligence Agency 中央情報局（米国）
CO₂	carbon dioxide 二酸化炭素
DPRK	Democratic People's Republic of Korea 北朝鮮
EU	European Union 欧州連合
FAO	Food and Agriculture Organization 食糧農業機関（国連）
FBI	Federal Bureau of Investigation 連邦捜査局（米国）
FRB	Federal Reserve Bank 連邦準備銀行（米国）
GDP	gross domestic product 国内総生産
GMT	Greenwich Mean Time グリニッジ標準時
GOP	Grand Old Party 共和党（米国）（＝Republican Party）
G8	Group of Eight (Major Industrial Countries) 先進8ヵ国
GWR	Guinness World Records ギネス世界記録
HIV	human immunodeficiency virus ヒト免疫不全ウイルス
IAEA	International Atomic Energy Agency 国際原子力機関（1957年発足）
IBRD	International Bank for Reconstruction and Development 国際復興開発銀行（通称World Bank [世界銀行]）
ID	identification 身分証明
IEA	International Energy Agency 国際エネルギー機関（OECDの下部組織、1974年設置）
ILO	International Labor Organization 国際労働機関（1919年設立）
IMF	International Monetary Fund 国際通貨基金（1945年発足）
IP	Internet Protocol インターネットプロトコル（コンピューターをインターネットに直接接続するためのプロトコル）
IQ	intelligence quotient 知能指数
IRA	Irish Republican Army アイルランド共和国軍（北アイルランドのカトリック系反英地下組織）
IWC	International Whaling Commission 国際捕鯨委員会
JAL	Japan Airlines Corporation 日本航空株式会社
JETRO	Japan External Trade Organization 日本貿易振興機構
JSDF	Japan Self-Defense Forces 自衛隊（日本）
JST	Japan Standard Time 日本標準時
LCC	Low Cost Carrier(s) 格安航空会社
LED	light-emitting diode 発光ダイオード
LSI	large-scale integration 大規模集積回路（コンピューター）
MRSA	methicilin-resistant staphylococcus aureus メチシリン耐性黄色ブドウ球菌
MVP	most valuable player 最優秀選手（野球）
NASA	National Aeronautics and Space Administration 航空宇宙局（米国）
NATO	North Atlantic Treaty Organization 北大西洋条約機構（1949年設立）
NG	no good 失敗
NGO	nongovernmental organization 非政府組織
NPO	nonprofit organization 民間非営利組織

ODA	Official Development Assistance 政府開発援助（日本）
OECD	Organization for Economic Cooperation and Development 経済協力開発機構
OHP	overhead projector オーバーヘッドプロジェクター
OPEC	Organization of the Petroleum Exporting Countries 石油輸出国機構
PLO	Palestine Liberation Organization パレスチナ解放機構（1974年から国連オブザーバー）
RBI	run(s) batted in 打点（野球）
ROK	Republic of Korea 大韓民国
RSPCA	Royal Society for the Prevention of Cruelty to Animals（英国）王立動物虐待防止協会（1824年設立）
SDI	Strategic Defense Initiative 戦略防衛構想（米国）
START	Strategic Arms Reduction Treaty 戦略兵器削減条約
TEPCO	Tokyo Electric Power Company 東京電力株式会社
TOEIC	Test of English for International Communication トーイック
TPP	Trans-Pacific Partnership 環太平洋連携協定
UN	United Nations 国連
UNCTAD	United Nations Conference on Trade and Development 国連貿易開発会議（1964年設立）
UNESCO	United Nations Educational, Scientific and Cultural Organization 国連教育科学文化機関、ユネスコ
UNHCR	United Nations High Commissioner for Refugees 国連難民高等弁務官事務所（1951年設立）
UNICEF	United Nations Children's Fund 国連児童基金（1946年設立）
UNIDO	United Nations Industrial Development Organization 国連工業開発機関
UNSC	United Nations Security Council 国連安全保障理事会
UNU	United Nations University 国連大学
VIP	very important person 重要人物
WHO	World Health Organization 世界保健機関（国連、1948年設立）
WTO	World Trade Organization 世界貿易機関（1995年発足）
WWF	World Wide Fund for Nature 世界自然保護基金（1961年 英国で発足）

日本の主要官庁名

内閣官房	Cabinet Secretariat
内閣府	Cabinet Office
防衛省	Ministry of Defense
総務省	Ministry of Internal Affairs and Communications
法務省	Ministry of Justice
外務省	Ministry of Foreign Affairs of Japan
財務省	Ministry of Finance Japan
文部科学省	Ministry of Education, Culture, Sports, Science and Technology
厚生労働省	Ministry of Health, Labour and Welfare
社会保険庁	Social Insurance Agency
農林水産省	Ministry of Agriculture, Forestry and Fisheries
経済産業省	Ministry of Economy, Trade and Industry
国土交通省	Ministry of Land, Infrastructure, Transport and Tourism
観光庁	Japan Tourism Agency
海上保安庁	Japan Coast Guard
環境省	Ministry of the Environment
警察庁	National Police Agency

TEXT PRODUCTION STAFF

edited by	編集
Hiroko Nakazawa	中澤 ひろ子

English-language editing by	英文校閲
Bill Benfield	ビル・ベンフィールド

cover design by	表紙デザイン
Nobuyoshi Fujino	藤野 伸芳

text design by	本文デザイン
Ruben Frosali	ルーベン・フロサリ

CD PRODUCTION STAFF

narrated by	吹き込み者
Howard Colefield (AmE)	ハワード・コルフィールド (アメリカ英語)
Jennifer Okano (AmE)	ジェニファー・オカノ (アメリカ英語)

Meet the World 2023 English through Newspapers
メディアで学ぶ日本と世界2023

2023年1月20日　初版発行
2023年2月15日　第2刷発行

編著者　若有　保彦

発行者　佐野 英一郎

発行所　株式会社 成 美 堂
　　　　〒101-0052東京都千代田区神田小川町3-22
　　　　TEL 03-3291-2261　　FAX 03-3293-5490
　　　　http://www.seibido.co.jp

印刷・製本　三美印刷株式会社

ISBN 978-4-7919-7271-5　　　　　　　　　　　Printed in Japan

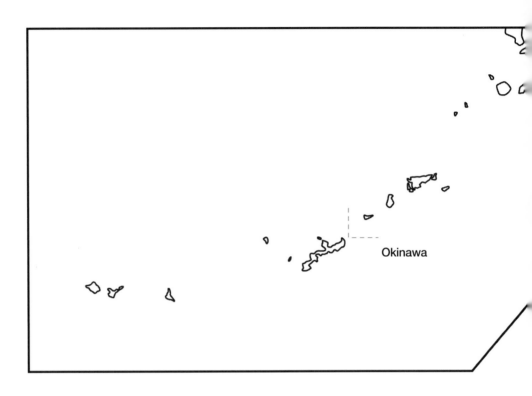

Okinawa

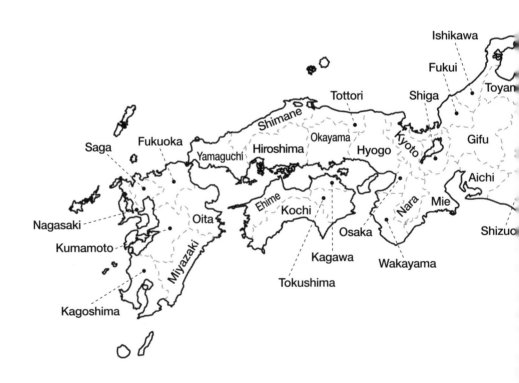

Ishikawa
Fukui
Toyan
Tottori
Shiga
Shimane
Okayama
Kyoto
Gifu
Saga
Fukuoka
Yamaguchi
Hiroshima
Hyogo
Nagasaki
Ehime
Nara
Aichi
Oita
Kochi
Mie
Kumamoto
Osaka
Shizuo
Miyazaki
Kagawa
Wakayama
Kagoshima
Tokushima